Prai
All I Need To
Manufacturing I Lea

"Must reading for anybody manufacturing anything."
Bill Jasper, President
Dolby

"Wraps up more lessons in a one-hour read than all the high-priced seminars you could attend."
John Guffey, Chief Executive Officer
Coltec

"If you're looking for an overview of current manufacturing concepts in an easy-to-read format, I suggest *All I Need To Know About Manufacturing I Learned In Joe's Garage*."
Jim Treece, Senior Correspondent
Business Week Magazine

"Insightful–magic–easily understood and retained."
Mary Osmolski, Director, Stanley Production System
Stanley Works

"Creates retained understanding of huge impact of creating and manufacturing a cost effective, quality product."
Ronald F. McKenna, Chief Operating Officer
Sundstrand Aerospace

"Refocused our organization on fundamentals of World Class Manufacturing."
Dale Philippi, Vice President
Eureka

"Excellent. Universally applicable to all manufacturing processes."
Robert A. Lutz, Vice Chairman
General Motors

"Really helped change the thinking in our manufacturing organization."
Mike Eagle, Vice President, Manufacturing
Eli Lilly

ALL THAT MATTERS ABOUT
QUALITY
I LEARNED IN JOE'S GARAGE

High Quality
Made Simple

WILLIAM B. MILLER   VICKI L. SCHENK

♦ Bayrock Press ♦

Contents

All That Matters About Quality...

***Great Accomplishments Are
Possible With Attention
To Small Beginnings***

WHAT DO I DO NOW?

I have always been good (or lucky) at extricating myself from difficult situations, but this time was different. The path on which I had set us for our weekend journey seemed to lead straight to the edge of a precipice.

It was seven o'clock on Sunday morning. The garage looked like a mobile home park after a visit from a black funnel cloud. Pieces of two-by-fours and plywood were scattered around the floor. Numerous sizes and colors of carpet remnants created an incomplete but intriguing mosaic. Loose nails and screws added to the image of chaotic destruction.

I walked to the door leading to the back yard and surveyed the scene on the patio and large lawn. The carnage was neater, although no more comprehensible. A team of mad sculptors apparently had worked feverishly on a dozen or so creations from a new school of modern art, then had abruptly vanished, leaving behind their works in various stages of completion.

It was hard to believe that I had actually planned this mess. Or, more accurately, had set in motion the events that had produced it. Things were not supposed to be working out this way. By now the project should have been well on its way to being an unqualified success that would make the participants happy and possibly become famous enough to receive an admiring writeup in the local newspaper.

I was mad and I felt like breaking something. Instead I let out a single deep sigh of exasperation. That was all the disappointment I was going to allow myself. I didn't know how I was going to resolve either the condition of the project or the new crises that had come pouring through the Internet in the past several hours, but there had to be something I could do. I am a world class fire-fighter and crisis manager. Everybody says so. Sometimes they mean it as a compliment; sometimes they don't.

I unclenched my jaw and fists and went back into the house to get a pad and pen to make notes. I was going to be prepared for action by the time my guests arrived at ten o'clock.

My name is Joe. It's my **6** *m* ★!! garage that's in need of a disaster cleanup crew. And this is my story about quality—a work in progress with an uncertain ending.

*All Things Are Difficult
Before They Are Easy*

**Understanding Is More
Than The Sum Of The Facts**

THE FIRST STEP

It all started last Wednesday evening. The sun was dimming to a purple memory on the horizon when the doorbell rang. "Joe," Virginia called down the hallway, "Sandy and Ralph are here." I clicked off the radio, jumped up from my desk chair, grabbed my file folders and writing pad, and headed for the living room.

Sandy used to work at Garrett Gear in one of my Operations departments, then got a promotion to move to Ralph's employer, a competitor with a local plant. They are about the same age, mid-thirties. A while back they helped me and a team of neighbors build shelves in my garage. That was an experience I'm not liable to forget in this lifetime, believe me.

I was nervous. I don't get nervous! Of course, the last time Sandy and Ralph were invited over for one of my projects, I made a total fool of myself (although I didn't think so at the time). I was not eager for another opportunity to feel like I had unknowingly walked around all day made up with white grease-paint and a bright red spherical nose. I took several deep breaths and let them out slowly. A little trick Virginia brought home from her yoga class; it works most of the time to calm me down.

I took one of the plum wing chairs across from Ralph and Sandy who were seated on the coordinating sofa. Virginia served coffee and tea while I explained the notion of building cat furniture to my guests.

I described the two kinds of cat furniture that the neighbors were interested in—scratching posts and climbing trees. A scratching post is a wood 4x4 wrapped with sisal rope and carpet, standing upright on a sturdy base. They come in various heights. Cat climbing trees have a central vertical post, also a 4x4, attached to which are horizontal limbs sticking out like arms of a Saguaro cactus. The limbs are anything that a cat might enjoy playing or lying on or around: platforms, platforms with sides, round or square tunnels, tiny houses with windows and doorways, anything you can think of. The limbs are sometimes supported by additional vertical members attached to the same base as the central post. All pieces are covered with carpet. Climbing trees range from three to eight feet high. Frequently a scratching post is incorporated into the cat tree design as a vertical supporting member. Climbing trees are sometimes adorned with fuzzy balls or cubes hanging from the limbs, so a cat can lie on a platform and play with a ball dangling above his head.

I showed them catalog pictures of cat furniture. Sandy nodded. "I have a cat," she said. "As well as a dog. I'm familiar with these things." She poured another cup of coffee from the thermal pot and stirred sugar into it.

"Me too," Ralph said. "Three cats. One climbing tree. They each want their own. Mia and I haven't succumbed yet. Darn stuff is incredibly expensive. Hundreds of dollars for the nice ones. And all they are basically is scrap wood covered with carpet remnants." He grimaced.

I couldn't have asked for a better setup for my pitch. I explained that several kids and their parents had come calling three weeks ago. They knew what my day job was and they assumed I wasn't ignorant about making things. They wondered if I could teach them to build scratching posts and climbing trees inexpensively. They were willing to supply the labor and pay for materials. What they needed was somebody who could figure out how to design and manufacture these relatively simple products. Me.

Sandy grinned. "And you couldn't very well tell them that although you were Vice President of Ops for a company making complex machinery, you couldn't teach your neighbors to glue carpet pieces and rope to wood, then fasten the wood together into a cat toy. I understand." Sandy is very competent, but tact has never been her strong suit. It was nice to see that she hadn't changed since leaving Garrett. It meant she was doing well in her new job and enjoying it.

"You've got it," I agreed. "A group of parents and kids are coming over Saturday morning to build cat furniture." I opened one of my folders and gave them materials lists and drawings to look at. They sat forward on the sofa and spread out the information on the glass-topped coffee table.

"These things are more complicated than you would imagine," I said. "At least climbing trees are. Consider the impact of a couple of fifteen-pound cats jumping off and on a cat tree platform four feet above the floor. The cat tree has to remain upright; it can't topple over into your TV set. Or on top of your miniature poodle. Consider the carpet covering the frame. It can't snag their claws or disintegrate into threads that are messy and dangerous for cats to eat. And so on and so on."

I handed them the contents of another folder (my word processing and design software have recently gotten strenuous workouts). "Here are the design specifications. Twenty pages. The materials lists and design drawings are based on these."

They were absorbed in reading for a while, swapping pages back and forth. Virginia came in to refill the drink pots and set down a plate of homemade oatmeal-raisin bars, then returned to phone calls in the kitchen (she was coordinating production activities for a local theater company). Ralph and Sandy passed on snacks, but I fed my jitters four goodies and two cups of coffee. I really, **really** didn't want them to find any mistakes. At least not on their first exposure to the work of the new Joe! Not wanting to appear anxious, I focused on the near-full moon visible through a crack in the drapes. Idly wondered if my cat furniture project in three days was going to be subject to the occult forces—whatever they were—of a full moon.

Ralph finally spoke. "This is nice work. I don't see anything you've left out. You've designed better furniture than pet stores sell. Our cats can knock over the climbing tree when they get into one of their playing frenzies, so we don't have anything breakable near it."

"I like the emphasis on low cost," Sandy added. "Fasteners and brackets, for instance. You've got a good selection that will do the job for which they are needed—provide adequate support without over-engineering and excessive cost. And you've specified a rustproof low-grade finish. Don't need chrome or anything pretty—nobody ever sees the fasteners, since they are covered with carpet."

She and Ralph exchanged glances. I knew what was coming next. I hoped.

"So why are we here?" she asked. "Is it the production issues? Building the furniture from these designs? Because I'm not sure we can help you. Our company doesn't do things the way Garrett does. As you know. We would probably just be disruptive." She held my eyes, but Ralph kept his gaze on the table. There it was—the issue I was simultaneously dreading and waiting for.

"No," I replied. "At least not the way you mean the question." I surreptitiously took a deep breath. "You are sitting across from a new Joe. The shelf-building project in my garage was very educational. Garrett's production processes now are different than when you were with us. I'm not saying we don't have implementation problems—a few pretty serious ones, in fact—but we are on the right track. I'm totally comfortable with your approach." They looked at each other again, and I thought maybe I saw a couple of small smiles.

I took a sip of coffee and went on. "Which is why I could use your assistance. If you have time. I know you are both busy and after the experience with the shelves have no reason to help me." This is another feature of the new Joe: humility.

"There are two major concerns I have about this cat furniture building project," I said. "Three if you count shepherding a dozen adults and kids so they can build the stuff without getting frustrated or smashing a finger. But I don't mean that. The first major concern is getting the job done within the allotted time and cost. After all, that is the whole point of the project—helping people build cat scratching posts and climbing trees so efficiently that it's a better deal to them than shelling out a hundred bucks or more at the pet store. To expand on your comment a while ago, Sandy, I am not interested in demonstrating that I know less about efficient design and production than the people who make the stuff in those catalogs." I pointed to the pages lying on the coffee table.

"I get that," Sandy said. "What is the second concern?"

Before I could reply, Buzzy made his usual regal entrance. Buzzy is our 15-year old Himalayan. Himalayans are long-haired cats with a ratio of soft long fur to body volume of approximately 100 to 1. A skeleton in a huge muff. Some are aloof, and some are cuddly. Buzzy is both—or either. Tonight he wasn't being particularly social, so he took a place beside my chair, out of reach of the visitors. He lay down slowly; at his advanced years, he doesn't move well or quickly. And he definitely has given up jumping. Our last cat tree went to our son and his wife three years ago.

I stroked Buzzy, then said "Quality" to Sandy's query about my second concern. I described my odyssey to pet stores, checking out different brands of cat furniture. I ordered pieces from catalogs. I discovered that some furniture is obviously crummy. Bad designs such as bases so small that units tip over easily. Poor materials such as mismatched carpet segments. Poor production such as sloppy seams joining two ends of a carpet piece wrapped around a post.

Other furniture has more subtle defects. A platform attached slightly askew to the central post—not quite level, but not evident unless you look at it from the right angle. Or design choices I wouldn't make, such as failing to carpet the bottom of a platform. A minor thing to the manufacturer, I said, "but as a customer, would you be pleased that they had saved a few cents in the production of a hundred dollar item and made it cosmetically ugly in the process?"

"Why is that a quality issue?" Ralph deadpanned. "If they designed the piece without a carpeted platform bottom and then built it as they designed it? Isn't that actually high quality? That they did exactly what they said they were going to do?"

Ralph's company sells very high quality machines, so I knew he was merely testing me. I let my eyes wander over the springtime desert painting above the sofa, depicting a budding palo verde tree above yellow and pink cactus flowers, while I decided how to respond succinctly.

"It goes to customer requirements," I replied after about a minute. "*True* customer requirements. Quality is compliance with requirements, true. Companies that don't carpet all surfaces of cat furniture would claim that customers don't care if everything is carpeted—that their furniture as it is satisfies customers' aesthetic requirements—and that cats won't be climbing on the bottom of platforms and certainly don't care. Their products therefore meet customer requirements. But they are wrong."

I was getting warmed up now—quality is my new passion. Unconsciously I stood and began walking around the room. Buzzy turned his head so his eyes could follow me while his body remained motionless as a taxidermist's display.

"Let me tell you what the future holds for those smug companies." I pointed my finger pistol-style at an imaginary adversary. "Another company will come along with fully carpeted cat furniture. Maybe for the same price, maybe for a tiny bit more. Doesn't matter. In a short time, they will have grabbed more market share, 'cause customers will prefer their products. Whether their unit profit is slightly lower or not, they will sell a higher volume, making a higher total profit. And here is the kicker—their higher volume will soon enable them to buy carpet and other materials from their suppliers at lower prices. So, they will end up making a higher unit profit as well as a higher total profit. The company with the better product will actually make more money."

"People who buy solely from catalogs will be especially happy," I finished. "Catalog photos are deceptive, appearing to show all carpeted surfaces. Only after customers have had their credit cards charged and received their deliveries do they realize platform bottoms are not carpeted. They can't complain, since the catalog description doesn't say 'fully carpeted.' But they will be more careful with their future purchases, and they will be delighted to find another company that actually makes a high quality product."

I sat back down in my chair—caught my breath—waited for their reaction.

"You seem to have gotten religion," Sandy observed dryly.

"Why not?" I shot back. "Your company has been kicking Garrett's butt for years. Part of the reason is efficient manufacturing, but another part is quality. Your products are more attractive to customers. We do not intend for that to go on much longer." My passion had spilled over into my vocal volume, and I suddenly flashed on an image of myself as a black-garbed revivalist preacher chastising sinners in his congregation. I dropped my hands to my lap and leaned back in my chair, willing myself to be calm.

"An excellent conversation topic for an interesting discussion," Ralph commented quietly. "I doubt it will be as easy as you think for Garrett to dislodge us from the customers' hearts."

"No fighting, please, gentlemen," Sandy said pleasantly. "Let's stay focused on building cat furniture. Joe, it appears that you and we are finally—perhaps surprisingly—on the same page. Of the same book. What are you looking for us to contribute to this project? And I think I will have one of those bars." Ralph took one, too (Virginia uses molasses and plenty of raisins) and they munched as I responded.

I laid it out for them as succinctly as I could. I planned to have my hands full with the quality issue. I wanted my neighbors to build cat furniture for themselves that was every bit as good as products carried by pet stores and pet supply houses—in fact, better where it could be better. And, candidly, my interest in high quality was born in the recent past. I wasn't sure I knew how to create it, and I wanted to learn—firsthand. Sandy and Ralph could easily set up and run an efficient production operation that would leave me free to concentrate on quality. If they could see their way clear to do that, I would be very grateful for the favor.

They were silent for a few minutes, each with their own thoughts. Sandy spoke first. "I suppose you can count me in. It would be fun. Besides, I probably owe you something for the things you taught me. They weren't all wrong. By the way, these are really good!" She took another bar from the plate.

"I'll take that as a compliment—for both me and Virginia," I said. "How about you, Ralph?"

He didn't reply immediately. I figured he was debating the value of his time versus the opportunity to determine how much I actually knew about quality and how much of a dent Garrett could potentially make in his company's market share. I hoped curiosity would win out. He sipped his tea slowly while he concentrated. Then he nodded, apparently having made his decision, and looked at me.

"Okay," he said. "I would be happy to work with Sandy on the production elements while your emphasis is quality. I must say, however, that I do not think they are truly independent issues. In my company's view, they are integrated quite tightly."

"No argument there," I said quickly, although in truth it was a new idea to me. At least to the degree that Ralph seemed to be espousing it.

"Fine," Ralph said with a bit more enthusiasm. "You and we will work together in order to develop a total system. Our primary goal will be efficient production, and yours will be high quality. Is that correct?"

"Yes," I said simply. The impact of Ralph's clear summations provided a glimmer of why Sandy admired him enough to jump ship after the shelf project.

The three of us talked for about fifteen minutes longer. I filled them in on the logistics of my materials acquisitions and of the Saturday schedule. I discussed, and gave them copies of, the numerous emails sent and received about the project.

Shortly there was no more except to agree that they would arrive at the house on Saturday morning a half hour before the kids and their parents. After saying goodbye to Virginia, they shook my hand and left with smiles on their faces.

"How did it go?" my wife asked when we were alone in the kitchen. "I didn't hear any angry voices, and they seemed happy when they left. Were your concerns unfounded?" She was referring to my apprehension about the evening that I had earlier shared with her.

"I guess so," I said, then paused. "What I really mean is I hope so." I summarized the discussion for her. She is my best friend and adviser, and I value her input on everything. I mentioned Ralph's comment about production and quality interaction, and expressed my concern about other potential surprises waiting to jump out of the bushes.

When I had finished, she took my calloused hand between her soft palms. "The project will go fine, Joe. Everybody will get what they need. You're a leader, and you believe in the right things." *I do now. Only took most of my career to get there.* Virginia is the gravity that anchors me and the oxygen that sustains me.

She went on to bed while I decompressed with another two mugs of coffee and a large slice of strawberry-rhubarb pie. I am one of those people who can go to sleep immediately after downing a pot of caffeinated coffee. I'm not sure if that's a blessing or a curse.

I went back into my study/office and found an unused spiral notebook with a red cover that seemed appropriate for the importance of this project. Ralph's words about integrating production and quality were resonating in my mind. I thought other insights would probably arise during the course of the project, and I decided to record them in a journal that would comprise a conceptual history of the project. It was one of the best decisions I ever made.

I wrote Ralph's concept in my journal, then joined Virginia in bed, and we watched "Star Trek" for an hour. When I turned out the light and closed my eyes, I felt quite content. The evening with Sandy and Ralph had been a success, and I was sure the project would go equally smoothly on Saturday. My optimism turned out to be more than a little bit premature.

**Do Not Fear Going Forward;
Fear Only Standing Still**

NO TURNING BACK

Thursday and Friday were uneventful days at the plant. Joe Junior called three times, but he didn't leave a message or ask for a return call. Odd, but I chose not to worry about it. All machinery orders shipped on time (customers' definition of on time, not ours; we learned that lesson recently.) My thoughts kept straying to building cat furniture—especially as compared to building shelves.

The way we function in Operations did a screeching U-turn after the shelf building project in the garage. Sandy's leaving the company shook me up. My brain worked harder than it had in a decade as I analyzed how I had managed the shelf construction, the results of my management, and what I could have done differently. I surprised Virginia by reading books other than mystery novels. I visited other companies and spoke with hundreds of people. Then I began to implement changes in how our plant designed and built products—both for distributor stock orders and for custom orders.

We have made progress. As somebody once said about their health, we ain't well yet, but we sure are better. Our leadtimes, costs, and performance to commitments are the best they have ever been. We still flush away far too much money and time on rework and warranty claims, but I was hoping to attack the quality problems over the next twelve months. I knew quality would be at least as high a mountain to climb as productivity and performance had been.

Ralph's concept of integrating production and quality had my cerebrum in a tight grip. I wondered if it implied that Operations wouldn't have to go back to Square One to improve our quality. If we could build on the lessons I had learned during the shelf-building project and the subsequent successes we had so painfully achieved at the plant. An uplifting thought that—with coffee—carried me swiftly through the hours remaining until Saturday morning.

"Got your chocolate doughnuts, Sandy," I said, pointing to the box on the kitchen counter. As planned, she and Ralph had arrived at 8:30 on Saturday, half an hour before the neighborhood kids and parents who were going to do the actual construction of cat furniture.

"You remembered," she said as she poured a cup of coffee. "I'm impressed. This really is a new Joe." Ralph didn't say anything. He was absorbed in an almond bear claw which I knew was fresh as well as huge—Virginia and I don't skimp on morning pastries. I tell her that it proves my dedication to quality. She gives me a sharp-eyed look and laughs.

I explained my plan to start slow and simple. To build two articles: a short scratching post and a climbing tree with four arms, each being a platform on which a cat could lie. "Prototypes. The people will be divided into two teams—one for each article. They will learn to build the item, then they will divide into a larger number of teams and crank out different varieties of scratching posts and climbing trees." I explained that each participating household had an interest in a particular design, or two or three, of cat furniture. Following my approach, by mid-Sunday everybody would have created their desired products for themselves—rapidly and inexpensively. They would be happy, and I would be a hero. (I didn't see any need to mention the last point to Ralph and Sandy.)

"Prototypes are a good idea," Ralph said. "They allow for debugging of designs and production processes."

Sandy agreed. "You don't want to take a chance on a production method not working when somebody uses it. Even with skilled workers using correct equipment, there is no guarantee that the procedures they are asked to follow will build the product correctly. Unless the processes are tested and validated. Major processes, of course—excluding variations and minor processes that really are not critical to production performance."

My stomach attempted to crawl up my esophagus as I realized the implications of her comment. I calmly said that I had a final task to finish up, then poured a cup of coffee and, leaving them to finish their breakfasts, walked to my office in the back of the house. *There were only ten minutes until the people would start to arrive!*

I hurriedly located the file with my notes on cat furniture desired by each household that would be coming today. Mostly I had pictures torn from catalogs, with notations on preferences for dimensions, color, and so forth. I quickly confirmed that I had a problem. My prototyping didn't include some of the features desired—such as a carpet-covered house ('cat condo') or a dangling toy. In my desire to create simple prototypes, I had inadvertently failed to include all the processes that needed to be validated. I didn't need every product variation, but people surely did have to learn how to build a cat condo and then cover it seamlessly with carpet.

In five minutes more I had sketched a third prototype, located manufacturing instructions for the processes required, and inhaled all but a few molecules of the coffee. I set about restructuring the teams for the new prototype definitions. In ninety seconds, I had three columns on my pad:

Team 1	Team 2	Team 3
Ellis	Mary	Zeb
Brad (Ellis's son)	Ann	Roger
Melissa	Mickey	Luis
	Kim	Betty

I had barely finished the team reorganization when the first arrivals rang the doorbell. I quickly ran off copies of the team assignments, then headed down the hall to the front door. Halfway there I remembered my resolve to record things I learned in my journal. No time to get out the journal now, so I took a 3x5 index card from my shirt pocket (I always carry a few) and wrote Production prototyping—include all critical products & processes. Then I went to direct people into the family room for my presentation and discussion.

By 9:15 everyone had arrived, and by 9:30 they were sufficiently dosed with coffee, tea, and pastries to pay attention to what I had to say. Everybody knew why they were spending a day and a half of their weekend at my house. All they needed to hear were details of how they would outsmart the pet stores by building elegant cat furniture for a fraction of retail price.

Some teenagers and adults had come alone, and others were with family members. Both couches and all the chairs, including TV recliners, were occupied. Buzzy had been dozing on a recliner, but he is not fond of crowds; he had left. Ellis and Mary were the sole returnees from the shelf building project. They remained standing—Ellis stocky and balding, Mary tall and slender with curly hair—arms folded across their chests, faces carved in stone. Ellis's son Brad and Mary's daughter (who was so young I assumed she was here to watch rather than to do) were also expressionless. Everybody else looked happy and eager to start.

"Thanks for coming," I said. "I'm hoping that together we'll be able to produce scratching posts and climbing trees that your little furry friends will enjoy. Now, without further ado...." I distributed drawings illustrating the final products, assembly sequence, and materials operations such as carpet cutting. I gave them lists of materials we would be using, from major items like wood to minor items like screws, and showed them where materials were referenced on drawings.

I passed out manufacturing instructions for the three prototypes: written descriptions of the production steps to build the products, including time estimates for each step. I gave people plenty of time to look at everything as it circulated among them. Each team would later have all the time they needed to understand their documents fully, but I also wanted people to grasp enough now that they didn't feel overwhelmed.

I concluded by saying, "Now let's go to the garage and get our hands dirty." Ellis raised his hand and asked grimly, "Joe, shouldn't we wait for the others to show up? This group can't be everybody who is coming. I mean, based on how we built the shelves."

A momentary flash of annoyance hit me, but then I smiled—hopefully in a friendly way, not a Jack Nicholson way. "Ellis, thanks for asking that. Everyone we need is here. We're doing things differently down at the plant now, and I'm trying to incorporate those things here. I think you'll have an easier time today." *Wouldn't be difficult—last time he left convinced I was a candidate for capital punishment.*

"I hope so." He muttered something to Mary beside him, the other shelf building veteran. It was too low to hear, but I would have bet it was something like, "I'll believe it when I see it." That was fine with me. I had a point to prove today.

I led the group into the garage, switched on the ceiling fluorescents, and punched the button to open the overhead driveway door. Our house faces south, so there was bright light streaming in, but being from an angle it wouldn't blind anyone. And the multi-colored irises blooming in the front beds were better scenery than the inside of a garage door.

I had purchased three scratching posts and climbing trees to use as examples of the products we were going to produce. They were at the back of the garage by the workbench, away from the main production floor; the cars had been moved to the driveway a couple of days ago. I explained the concept of prototyping—we would build three prototypes in the garage, then break into the multiple teams required to construct the various models of cat furniture that everybody wanted. At that point production would move to the back yard.

"Where is the wood?" Mary asked. "Last time there was a big pile of lumber in the back yard." Her eight year old daughter looked apprehensive that her mom had asked the question so directly. There must have been a discussion at their home of the shelf project.

"We're doing things differently," I repeated curtly. I pointed to the neat stacks of boards at the side of the garage. "Delivered pre-cut. Placed where they are going to be used in here." *As Ralph had recommended during the shelf project.* Since we were now going to build three prototypes, I realized we would have to bring in some boards and carpet from the stacks set up in the back yard for the volume production. Those materials had also been pre-cut, although in standard sizes that for some low-volume products would require an additional cut or so. No problem. Everything was organized according to usage; even the bulk items were properly sorted and labeled.

"I'm impressed," she said admiringly. Second time I had heard that word today. *This is okay.* I calmed down.

"Thanks," I said sincerely. "The tools are in the right place, too. Let me show you." I walked them through the plan to build each prototype completely in place. "That might change when we build a higher volume of products, if there are standard components we would like to build in quantities larger than one. But we will do that sparingly. Basically we will build things as we need them." I glanced quickly at Sandy and Ralph. They were both nodding their heads.

I was on a roll now. I *had* learned a few things from the shelf building project! Walking jauntily, I took the three prototype teams to their production areas. I crisply reviewed the production processes and the manufacturing instructions for each prototype. Team 1 for the scratching post was closest to the driveway. Teams 2 and 3 were along the sides of the garage under backdrops of wall-size posters that adorn three sides of my garage. Behind Team 2 was a full-size depiction of Graham Hill's Formula One race car at the Monaco Grand Prix. Graham Hill was a legendary driver; he once lost his clutch on the second lap of a race and drove the remaining laps shifting by the engine sound, finishing third.

A Boeing 747 passenger plane (not full size) was landing behind Team 3, flaps extended, nose gear and four main landing gear trucks clearly visible. At the back of the garage above the workbench was a bright yellow Union Pacific locomotive—Centennial class; 6,600 horsepower. I like machines and other tangible things that you can see and feel. I suppose that's why I invested my life in manufacturing.

Sandy and Ralph had agreed to monitor production of the prototype climbing trees—Sandy had Team 2's tree with flat platforms and Ralph had Team 3's tree with a cat condo instead of two of the platforms, and a fuzzy cube hanging from the underside of one platform. I would oversee the whole operation and assist as required with the scratching post—which wouldn't be much—it was pretty easy to build.

A tall teenager named Luis accompanied me to the back yard and helped bring in the few materials for the third prototype, since he was on Team 3. In a few minutes, his team was humming smoothly along with the other two teams. It was a marvelous sight—compact production by people working cooperatively, against a backdrop of gorgeous flowers and a weeping willow tree on a sunny spring morning.

I went into the kitchen, made fresh coffee and tea, and poured it into insulated pots. I set the pots and accessories on the workbench for anybody who wanted a refill. Then I got a fresh cup of coffee for myself. I didn't want to be in the way of anybody who didn't need me, so I stood by the workbench and simply observed, admiring the clockwork precision of the scene before me.

For about five minutes. Then things started to go wrong.

WHAM! BANG! THUD!

Ellis, the Team 1 leader, was kneeling, spouting X-rated words, banging a three-foot length of 4x4 against the concrete floor. I recognized the 4x4 as the main pillar of the prototype scratching post. I sprinted over to see what had happened.

Ellis's young son Brad sat mute, staring at the floor. The other helper, a fifteen year old neighbor named Melissa, whispered, "He couldn't get the rope wound tight enough on the post. He needed two hands to pull the rope tight and hold it, but then the post would move 'cause Brad and I couldn't keep it steady, so the rope would slip, and… you know, it just wouldn't work." She shook her head. Her hair was auburn with a green stripe running through it. Not a fashion Virginia was likely to adopt, but it coordinated well with her pink shirt.

I saw where I had goofed. Twice, actually—once in the instructions, once in the design of how to attach the rope to the post. I led the frustrated threesome to the workbench, where we used the attached vise to hold the 4x4 post while we wrapped the rope tightly around it. We used heavy-duty staples to attach the rope to the post every few turns, instead of attaching it only once at the end as my design had shown.

I apologized to Ellis for my mistakes. "The instructions should have mentioned the vise. The design should have recognized that commercial producers of these things use machines to wrap the rope quickly and precisely. The machines can attach the rope once at the end. Humans need to attach it as they go so that it stays tight."

Ellis was mollified. He and the kids returned to the tasks of attaching the base to the post, and attaching a little sitting platform to the top of the post.

I pulled an index card from my pocket and wrote:

Instructions need to be complete and clear
Design should match capabilities & processes

My emotions were well beyond simmer, so I took a deep breath and reminded myself that finding errors was the reason we built prototypes. I returned the card to my pocket and turned my eyes away from the project that had been underway for less than half an hour and was already behind. Across the street a guy who had moved into the neighborhood last month with his family was attaching a nozzle to a garden hose. A big sponge, bucket, and rags were on the driveway at his feet, so I imagined car washing was on his Saturday list. His son was throwing a tennis ball for a Golden Retriever, who was proudly living up to the breed's name by bringing the ball back. Again and again. Just watching the dog made me tired. One door further down, two boys and two girls were bouncing and shooting a basketball in their driveway. At least somebody was having fun.

I turned around to confront another problem with the scratching post. Ellis, Brad, and Melissa were having difficulty centering and positioning the post on the two-foot-square plywood base. Obviously the same problem was going to occur with centering the little platform on the top of the post.

My instructions said to use a straight-edge and pencil to draw two lines on the base, each from a corner to the opposite corner, then position, and automatically center, the post by lining up its corners with the lines. The pencil lines would be covered from sight by the carpet on the base. Pretty clever, I thought when I wrote the instructions. Simple yet effective. After centering the post, you held it in place while you turned it upside down and used a power drill to drive five screws through the base, in roughly a square pattern around a center screw, to attach it to the post. It didn't matter exactly where the screws were placed—they were hefty screws, and would hold the base firmly—and you had to watch the post's position carefully only for the first two screws. After two screws were in, you were home free; the post was set in the correct position.

Out of the blue had come two things I hadn't considered. One, the vagaries of human opinion. If there were three people, there would be three opinions on precisely when the post had been centered. Secondly, ability and experience levels. I have big hands and years of experience with making things out of wood. Other people might have more difficulty than me with holding a post in position against a base while turning it over and driving screws—even if the tasks could be allocated among three people. In fact, you could probably make a case that more workers, of varying skills, made the task harder, not easier, than with one highly skilled worker.

As with the vise for winding the rope, the fix wasn't difficult. Using the intersection of the two diagonal lines on the base as a center point, we drilled a hole slightly smaller than the diameter of the screw through the plywood. We drew two intersecting diagonal lines on the bottom of the post and drilled a hole in the center of it. Then we made a mark one inch from the center hole along a diagonal line on both the base and the post, and drilled holes centered on the marks. The two center holes located the post in the center of the base, and the two other holes positioned the base and post correctly, to the precision required for our purposes, anyway. Ellis and Melissa each drove one screw through the base into the post to prove out the technique. They decided that they should give young Brad an opportunity to learn how to use a power tool, under strict supervision, so I left them to complete the attachment of the post to the base with the remaining three screws.

I went back into the kitchen. The ultimate results so far were pleasing—we were getting a quality product—but frustration with the unexpected problems had generated a burning desire for more sugar and caffeine. I finished a cheese Danish in four bites, not counting the portion Buzzy ate—of cream cheese, not flaky pastry. I sat on a stool at the breakfast bar and sipped coffee while I made another entry on my index card:

Make design easy to produce right, difficult to do wrong

I realized that the things I had done to improve scratching post production had a common theme. I added a heading to the card. It now read:

DESIGN FOR PRODUCTION

Instructions need to be complete and clear
Design should match capabilities & processes
Make design easy to produce right, difficult to do wrong

The index cards were turning out to be a good way to note the key actions I was taking to guarantee high quality cat furniture. Another thing I had done—eliminating opinion as a basis for deciding when the post was centered—occurred to me. It didn't seem to fit in the same category, so I wrote it on a different card:

Take subjectivity out of quality

I was aware too that the team and I had arbitrarily decided that visual accuracy was a satisfactory method for placement of the four holes we had drilled. The precision was fine for cat furniture, but it certainly wouldn't have been adequate for microchips or gene splicing. I wrote down another thought on the card, and added a heading. The card now said:

BASIC PRINCIPLES

Take subjectivity out of quality
Quality is meeting requirements for the particular product

I was now down to my last two index cards, so I headed for my office to replenish the supply in my pocket. While I was doing that, I heard the telephone ring in the kitchen. I looked around for the cordless phone handset that was usually on my desk or somewhere near me. Evidently in my burgeoning state of confusion I had left it someplace else. I let the kitchen answering machine take the call.

When I walked back through the kitchen to the garage, the red message light on the answering machine was blinking. It was Joe Junior saying he and Rachel **really** needed to discuss the matter he had called me about at the plant on Thursday and Friday. He said they would be coming over to discuss it this evening at about seven—unless we had something else planned. As if anything else could take precedence! The son and wife we loved had something to discuss that was too sensitive to describe in a message either at the plant or on our home telephone. *Of course we would see them!* I sighed and went back into the garage. It was becoming very clear that this day was not going to turn out as smoothly as I had anticipated.

*Reward Is In Proportion
To The Risk*

MORE DESIGN ISSUES

I paused on the top step leading into the garage. I was heartened at the effort obviously being expended by the three prototype teams. Ellis, Melissa, and Brad were engaged in an intense discussion around the scratching post. Sandy was helping Team 2 with building the prototype climbing tree with platforms. Ralph was involved with Team 3 building the climbing tree that included the cat condo. Late morning sun brightly illuminated the work space, but nobody was paying attention to the stunningly blue sky or the colorful foliage just outside the garage. People were heads down, concentrating, and their energy flowed in waves throughout the area.

I checked my watch, and disappointment surged through my cells. We were definitely supposed to be further along. I had planned a staggered effort, since the scratching post would be easier than the climbing trees. By now I expected the scratching post to be done. Its success would motivate the other teams, and the people from Team 1 could then assist with the other prototypes. Instead quality problems with the scratching post were delaying it and having a domino effect on the schedules of the other teams. *Just like the plant.* If you can do things right the first time, you can stay on schedule and meet your cost targets. If you have quality problems, everything suffers.

My musing was interrupted by Melissa homing in on me like a surface-to-surface missile. "We have a problem," she announced. "We screwed up." I followed her to the scratching post production space.

Ellis was angry but quiet. This time they had nobody to blame but themselves. The base was supposed to be attached to the post with 4" brass screws. The little platform on top of the post attached with 3" brass screws—made sense, since there would be less stress on the top platform, and 3" screws cost less than 4" screws. Unfortunately, the distinction had been lost on the team as they concentrated on the centering of the pieces and on the task of training young Brad. Only when they went to insert the final screw on the top platform—and discovered it was a 4" screw—did they notice they had accidentally used a 3" screw on the base.

"It's a prototype," I said philosophically. We decided that leaving the 3" screw in the base on this unit was better than replacing it in the same hole with the 4" screw, so they used the 4" screw on the top. The remaining issue was how to avoid making the same error when building future scratching posts.

"Make the instructions clearer," Ellis suggested. "Use color coding or highlighting or something to emphasize the difference in the screws."

"That would work," I agreed. It would be easy to modify the instructions for the production versions of the scratching post. Ellis had come up with a good solution.

"Why are there two different screw lengths?" Melissa asked. "It would be easier if we just used the same screw. We couldn't mess up."

"Cost," I said patiently. "Short screws cost less than long ones."

"I know *that*," she spat out. "I'm not stupid! But what's the cost of making mistakes? And if you bought the longer screws in larger quantities, wouldn't they cost less that way?"

It was like being hit with a two-by-four across the face. This kid had a bright future in production or engineering.

"Yes," I said. I didn't need to do the arithmetic. In addition to the purchase cost Melissa had identified, there were storage costs, handling costs, and probably other production costs that didn't spring to mind immediately. Design would be simpler, faster, and less costly, too. Fewer design errors as well as fewer production errors. A no–brainer.

"We'll use standard screws," I said. Ellis nodded. Melissa grinned with that teenage combination of triumph and guilt over besting an adult. Not to be outdone, Brad pumped his fist. "Yeah!" Smarting from the wounds, I remembered that I was, or was trying to be, a new Joe. I smiled weakly.

They moved on to the final task of carpeting the scratching post. I visually checked the other teams. Sandy was gesturing for me to come over to the Team 2 space. I gave her a One Moment signal, then jogged to the kitchen for more coffee to help digest the crow I was eating. And to record the screw decision on the **DESIGN FOR PRODUCTION** card.

I wrote **Minimal No. of Parts – Standard Parts**. Under that line, I noted — **standard means proven, known to work**. I replaced the card in my pocket and went to Sandy's area.

Team 2's prototype was a six-foot climbing tree with four platforms to be spaced equally vertically above the base. The uppermost platform would sit on top of the central post, with the others attached to it like a spiral staircase. The platforms were 14" square, enclosed by 3" sides. A short scratching post would run from the base to the second platform. All covered with carpet except for the rope wound on the scratching post.

"Mary has a question," Sandy said. "About placement of the posts. Basically about the stability of the whole thing."

"I do," Mary confirmed, looking directly into my eyes. She was a tall woman, only a couple inches shorter than me. Besides Ellis, she was the only person with shelf project experience. And, like Ellis, she had a problem today. *Great.*

"I like your design," she said. "It's cleaner—less clunky—than what the stores sell. Obviously cheaper to build. More features than the store stuff, with four platforms and them doubling as stairs. Or vice versa. A win-win-win situation. But…." She was hesitating. After the shelf project, I couldn't fault her for doubting me. I told her to go ahead.

"You see where the central post and the scratching post are attached to the base? Both on the same side of the base? On store trees, they are on diagonal corners. Better stability." Her daughter's eyes were even bigger than when Mom had asked about the wood inventory. *Whoa! Must have been quite a discussion at their home of Mr. Joe Hall's capabilities after the shelf project.*

She was right. In my excitement over adding the platform/stair combination feature in the clever spiral staircase arrangement, I had overlooked the importance of vertical post placement for balance. If a running cat jumped onto my cat tree on the side opposite the posts, the tree would tumble over as fast as a single-pin spare in a professional bowling tournament. Score a point for the store cat furniture designers.

My new humility was getting a workout from Ellis and Mary. I acknowledged the problem, and we set about correcting it. Wasn't difficult—relocating the posts and minor tweaking of the platform locations. We were done in fifteen minutes.

Even though the problem hadn't been a show-stopper, it was embarrassing to me and I was glad to see the pizza delivery van pulling up in front of the house. I called for a lunch break, and everybody stopped work to wash up.

People took their pizza slices on paper plates, paper towels, and sodas to the front lawn to eat in the fresh air under the powder blue sky. Ralph sat with his Team 3. Across the street Dad was washing the car's wheels and the Golden was still fetching the tennis ball. I knew bees were buzzing around out there—their population has been up this spring—so I opted for indoor dining. Sandy and I sat at the kitchen counter with our pizza and coffee. Sandy is as big a coffee hound as me, but she has the sense to drink decaf after her initial few cups.

"How's it going so far, Joe?"

"Not having a good day, Sandy," I said with probably a little too much self-pity in my voice. "I'm struggling. Too many design errors. We're already behind."

"Things will get better," she said in a neutral therapist's tone. "It's still only morning of the first day." She glanced at her watch. "Oops! Well, almost still morning."

"Can I pick your brains? I'm getting killed right out of the chute because the designs have quality problems. What do you know about developing a quality product design?" It was tough to ask this; growing up can be painful.

"Not much," she replied honestly. "Most of my work takes place after product design—or I provide input to product design—good processes, that sort of thing. But you seem to be getting a handle on that." She waved a hand towards the garage. "Speaking of which, I need to go work on the production of the tree with the new post locations. But I'll ask Ralph what he knows about product design." She hopped off her stool and headed out the door with her last slice of vegetarian pizza. I'm still a carnivore. I slowly finished my pepperoni slices while I tried to fight off pessimism that the day was getting away from me. By my last swallow, everybody else was finished, too, and back at their jobs in the garage. I went out to find Ralph and Team 3 to check on their progress.

On the way I passed Sandy discussing new procedures with Team 2 in the midst of idle tools and parts inventory. *Seconds and minutes gone forever.* Teams 1 and 3 were more heartening sights. In the sunlit area by the driveway, Ellis and company were concentrating on completing their scratching post. Under the 747, Team 3 was busy assembling a cat climbing tree. I dredged up a little smile as I said Hi to Ralph and Zeb Brown, my next door neighbor and leader of Team 3.

Ralph nodded politely while Zeb managed a gruff "Huh!" as a greeting. Zeb was named for Zebulon Pike, an explorer contemporary of Lewis & Clark and the discoverer of Pike's Peak. He's competent, he's big, and he likes to put on the image of a tough mountain man. His parents probably didn't know that Zebulon of mountain peak fame met with a humiliating end when he blew himself up with his own gunpowder during the War of 1812.

Speaking alternately, Zeb and Ralph filled me in on the team's progress. Their cat tree was the most complex of the prototypes. Attached to the central post were: two platforms, one braced by a scratching post, with fuzzy cubes dangling from them, plus a 'cat condo' that was like a large carpet-covered birdhouse with windows and an entrance big enough for a cat. The team had prepped the component pieces and was building subassemblies, moving towards final assembly. Ralph and Zeb explained that before beginning production they had taken some time to plan the production processes for maximum efficiency and short build time. They had even dealt with the same rope winding issue that had plagued Team 1, and had implemented a similar solution using a workbench vise.

I was impressed at the thoroughness of their efforts— except they hadn't thought of the interim stapling of the rope on the scratching post to facilitate keeping it tight during the winding. I explained how Team 1 and I had worked that out. They agreed it was a better way. Which gave me an idea.

"I'll write it up as a standard process," I said, "with standard instructions. Everybody will do the rope winding the same way." Ralph, Zeb, and the rest of the team agreed. Back to the kitchen I went for a caffeine refill, and then to my office.

I clicked on a local radio station that plays commercial-free blocks of oldies on Saturdays. On my computer I generated a standard "Rope Winding Process." I revised instructions for the prototypes to reference this Process instead of including it verbatim in each set of instructions. That was a better approach for at least two reasons. People could be trained on it as a standard process; improvements to it could be made to a central document instead of to numerous sets of instructions. *This is good.* My morale inched up a bit.

I printed copies for the teams. Before going back to the garage, I added to my **DESIGN FOR PRODUCTION** card:

Standard processes: best practices
Standard instructions—referenced, not repeated

I dropped off a Standard Rope Winding Process sheet, and the revised complete instruction set, with Team 1. They were almost done with the prototype scratching post, and I realized I would have to think about how to redeploy the team in a different way than I had planned. Team 2 was behind to schedule—currently still talking instead of doing—and Team 3 might or might not be behind. *Would have been a whole lot easier if everybody had stayed on schedule. Yeah—would have been nice if they hadn't run into quality problems due to my designs and instructions.*

Enough remorse for now. I gave Team 3 their copy of the standard winding process and their revised instructions, then turned to go check up on Sandy's progress with Team 2. Before I could move, Ralph quietly took me aside and said, "Joe, we're going to catch up with the schedule. But I anticipate some other problems. Could you come back as soon as you can?" In response to my puzzled look, he whispered cryptically, "I can't do this alone. The team has some serious internal disagreements." I said I would be back as soon as possible. *Not good. This is really not good.*

My mood brightened a bit when Sandy said Team 2 had finished their discussions and were about to resume production with the revised designs and manufacturing instructions. They wanted to review their plans with me. Through some diplomatic sleight of hand, Sandy had transformed Mary into the team presenter. Mary was a bit nervous, but she had herself under control. With a last glance back at Graham Hill intent on steering through a hairpin turn, she left her position at the wall and walked to the front of the group.

She showed me the design pages they had red-lined with changes. And assembly illustrations similarly marked up. She walked me through the minor revisions to assembly sequence.

"We also marked up the written instructions. Kim took care of that." Kim was a black-haired geeky kid with braces who rapidly and flawlessly described the revised manufacturing instructions, including a checklist for verifying that the manufacturing instructions were complete and clear.

"Your instructions were excellent, but we added a couple pieces of information," Kim said wearing an apologetic expression. "Such as particular skill levels a person had to possess in order to do a certain task." That comment and a checklist sounded like pretty advanced concepts for a home project, so I glanced over at Sandy. Her expression didn't change, but her eyes twinkled a little.

Well, I might have been able to find fault with what they had done—if I had a week—but now I was simply overwhelmed with the quality of the work. I asked what was next.

"Building it," Mary said firmly. "Assuming you're ready to turn us loose to get back on schedule?" Sandy nodded slightly.

I said "Yes," thanked them for their progress, and—pretending not to see Ralph's beseeching stare from the Team 3 area— returned to a stool at the kitchen counter. I consumed a raspberry Danish with my left hand (alone—Buzzy doesn't like fruit preserves) while I wrote an index card with my right:

PRODUCTION INSTRUCTIONS

All designs and processes documented
   – graphically and in simple writing
Include everything needed to build it well
   – e.g. resource capabilities, necessary steps,
    materials & supplies
Checklist to make sure nothing is left out

I ate the final crumbs of my Danish, then went to see what Ralph's hairball was.

Learn To Unlearn Your Learning

DESIGN IS NOT ENOUGH

I could see the fight starting from the doorway into the garage. In the Team 3 area a short wiry man was firing a hailstorm of irrational insults at big red-bearded Zeb towering over him. Zeb's placid countenance was gradually tightening and coloring. I had to do something before the little guy became either an involuntary projectile or a stain on the floor. I hustled my way through the spectators and positioned myself between them—I'm no Zeb, but I'm not a small man myself.

With some encouragement from me, they were able to talk about their problem in normal tones, and the other teams returned to work. Turned out Zeb and Roger had a disagreement about the cat condo that was now almost ready for attachment to the tree after Roger had finished its construction.

"The walls are square to the floor," Roger said. "They meet specifications. Anyone can see that."

"Actually, anybody can see that they aren't square," Zeb retorted. "And this proves it." He held a carpenter's square against the condo's floor and one of the walls. There was indeed a tiny gap at the 90° intersection of the tool's arms.

"Are you kidding?" Roger said, his voice starting to rise again. "This is for a CAT, not the space shuttle! It's fine!"

"This never should have happened," Zeb said. "You built it wrong when it was just as easy to build it right. You should have used one of these when you laid it out and screwed the pieces together." He held up the carpenter's square.

I hoped I saw a diplomatic solution instead of imposing Truth on them, which I still tend to do to people far too often. "I think the issue is how to decide whether the walls are square." They agreed. I gambled and asked Roger whether he wanted to use a measuring tool or his eyeball—and what he wanted people to do when they built more cat condos later today or tomorrow. Should everyone judge the squareness with their own individual eyesight?

"An objective tool is better," he consented. "I just wish I had known how you were going to judge me before I finished building it."

Zeb apologized and they set about figuring out how they were going to proceed from this point. The team was getting close to attaching the condo carpet covering and finishing the basic climbing tree structure. I wondered how they were going to fix the condo—or if they were. Fortunately, we were still in the prototyping stage.

I walked to the workbench and made out a new card:

INSPECTION

Measure to objective standards known to all
Use agreed-upon measuring tool/process

Zeb and Roger had agreed in this instance that the condo

inspection should be in accordance with the specification for the walls to be perpendicular, but I realized there was a general principle here too, so I added another line:

Inspection standards consistent with specifications
   - include all specifications that must be met

I was about to return the cards to my pocket when I realized Zeb had made a good point when he suggested using the carpenter's square in construction of the cat condo as well as in the inspection. I made up a new card, one that possibly was going to have many entries before the weekend was over:

PRODUCTION PROCESS

Production process should reduce chance of errors
   - ideally process designed to eliminate errors
Production process consistent with inspection methods
   - products built with process will pass inspection
Approved process documented and explained clearly

Virginia keeps recipes on cards in a box a foot long. I wondered if by Sunday evening I was going to need as large a box for my cards. Quality was a bigger topic than I had imagined. No wonder we hadn't yet cracked that nut at the company. The effort, however, would be justified. Every delay and cost problem today could be traced to poor quality or poor communication about quality. It was the same way at the plant.

I turned to find that Ralph had come up behind me. "You dodged a bullet, you know," he said quietly. In a similarly low voice, I asked what he meant.

"It's essential that production meets design specifications. But the real goal is to satisfy the customer. Maybe Roger was right and the walls were square enough for the actual customer requirements. Maybe the specs or Zeb's inspection technique were too constraining. Maybe there should have been an acceptable deviation from 90 degrees."

I pondered his comment for a millisecond or two before saying, "Not a chance. Down that road lies disaster. You start watering down the quality requirements and that never stops, when actually the marketplace and the customers are continually demanding higher quality. Or at least wanting it after they have seen it from one of your competitors. Besides—as Zeb said—high quality doesn't cost any more if you build it into the production process. And it's not like Zeb wanted to spend ten thousand bucks on laser equipment to verify that the walls were 90 degrees instead of 89.995 degrees. A simple carpenter's square was the perfect solution for both production and inspection of a cat climbing tree."

"You're probably right," Ralph said agreeably and walked back to the Team 3 area. *Testing me again. Won't work—Garrett has learned this lesson—we just need to figure out how to implement it."*

My next visitor was a smiling Ellis informing me that Team 1 had finished and inspected their prototype scratching post. I followed him to where Melissa and Brad were standing proudly beside their product. The team had done a nice job. The base and top platform were attached securely. The carpet pieces were matched and the seams were almost unnoticeable. Ellis showed me how they had used a carpenter's square (*Yes!*) to verify that the platform and base were square to the center post. As the finishing touch, he showed me the inspection steps on the instructions that he had initialed, as Team Leader, indicating that the inspections had been performed.

I thanked them sincerely for a job well done, then led the

three back to the Team 3 area, where I intended to add them to that team. It was obvious that Sandy and Team 2, having gotten the design behind them, were now ripping off progress in big chunks whereas Zeb was still trying to get his people flying in formation instead of in all directions of the compass. Halfway across the garage, inspiration lit up my mind. I jogged to the wall by the doorway where there is a white board on which I write notes to myself using erasable markers. I lifted the board off its hooks, carried it to the Team 1 area, wiped it clean with a rag, and created an **INSPECTION STATUS** board on which I recorded the activity and 100% results from Team 1's first output. I leaned it against the wall beside the prototype; I would figure out a better display approach this evening. It looked good. I was hoping that the concept would help us keep track of the progress towards attainment of quality in production of cat furniture—and improve the quality by monitoring it in real time as events occurred. There was a smattering of applause as I jogged back to the Team 3 area. *Even better. The white board, like any system, would work only if people believed in it and used it.*

My good humor quickly evaporated like ice chips in Death Valley. Zeb and Roger were going at it again. This time the problem was a platform Roger had attached to the central post. It was the second platform and it was obviously leaning at a slight angle—not truly horizontal—probably by only a couple degrees, but enough to be apparent to the human eye. Roger was beyond claiming that his work was fine for a cat. He had something else on his overwrought mind now.

"I've never heard of a freakin' spirit level!" he screamed up at Zeb. "I work in a coffeeshop! I only volunteered for this because I can't afford the stupid stuff at the pet store!" Zeb was wearing a curious expression, like a child who encounters a penguin in the zoo for the first time and can't believe what he is seeing. It all made sense to me now—this error and Roger's mistake with the cat condo. He knew nothing about woodworking, yet I and everybody else had assumed his presence conveyed a degree of competence. Big mistake.

Easy mistake to fix, however. Under the cover of merging Teams 1 and 3, Zeb and I casually inquired about people's skills, then assigned them to appropriate tasks. Ellis fixed the platform. Roger gratefully helped with sanding. All was good.

I glanced at my watch. Two problems immediately popped into my mind. One, I had not had a cup of java in over an hour. Two—and probably more important, although my nervous system didn't think so—it wasn't clear that people were going to be able to go home at four o'clock, as I had promised them when I arranged this shindig. I was looking at some schedule juggling and replanning. As my mother said, however, first things first—I headed for the kitchen. On the way I passed Sandy and Mary both gesturing that Team 2 wanted to see me. I guiltily shook them off, making hand signals that I hoped indicated I would return soon. I was out of control and knew I needed a break.

I was halfway through an old-fashioned cake doughnut, which are great for coffee dipping, when Virginia came into the kitchen. "Those things are going to kill you."

"I thought we agreed that they were okay in moderation."

"Moderation? How many have you had today? Five? Ten?"

"Not ten," I said defensively. "This will be my last one."

"It better be, or you'll get tofu for dinner." She smiled to let me know that she was kidding. I nodded and finished the doughnut in two bites before she could take it away.

The sugar high cleared my mind to click on the import of the events with Roger: people's qualifications and skills mattered. You had to have the right resources for a task in order to get it done correctly, the first time, on the planned schedule. I wrote a new card:

QUALITY - RESOURCES

Align resource capabilities with tasks to be done
− verified/certified capabilities

I included the second line because at the plant it wouldn't be fair to customers if people were assigned to tasks without objective certification of their qualifications to perform those tasks—also that task complexity and planned cycle times were consistent with people's levels of skills. I knew in theory the company trained people adequately and matched task assignments with skills and expertise. I wondered how objectively and quantitatively we put theory into practice. Finding out would be on my list of things to do Monday morning. A few people, out of thousands, asked to do jobs they couldn't do well in the allotted time could blow the plant's schedule, cost, or quality attainment. A truly sobering thought.

Refreshed—back to the garage—to Team 2, who had made more progress than ol' Graham, still stuck in his hairpin turn. Mary and Sandy wanted the team to demonstrate their inspection procedures. Their climbing tree, which had the four staircase platforms, was assembled and ready for the carpet covering. Mary had assigned the demonstration to a pony-tailed brunette named Ann. I thought getting team members actively involved in presentations was cool.

"We wanted to do the inspection of the assembled frame before we carpeted it," Ann said. "In order to correct any errors in attachment of platforms—looseness, squareness, levelness, whatever—before the carpet was glued on. For two reasons. One, not having to pull off carpet to fix something. Two, we'll get a more accurate inspection result if we measure things like squareness before the carpet is on." She raised her eyebrows. I nodded that I got the idea. On the distant horizon of my mind, alarm bells chimed faintly. I ignored them and listened to Ann. "We did the same thing with the platforms. They were inspected before and after attachment to the post." I nodded again.

They walked me through their inspection process. They had used simple tools like a tape measure, carpenter's square, and spirit level, but had been thorough. Including moving the cat tree to a location on the garage floor that measured as truly level. "It wouldn't have made much sense," Ann said, "to have measured a platform's levelness with the entire cat tree sitting on a non-level surface." I could tell she was proud they had thought of this nuance. I was, too, and I told them so.

Finally—not unexpectedly—they showed me their revised inspection instructions. "Much better than mine," I admitted. *No point in not being honest when somebody has done good work, even if your ox was gored by their work.* "Yours weren't wrong," Mary jumped in, "we just made them more precise." I told her my ego wasn't bruised beyond repair, then asked if I could borrow their document for a while. The alarm bells in my mind were now clanging loudly. She smiled, handed me the inspection procedures, and I headed for the Team 3 area.

Team 3 was motoring along in high gear. Zeb said Ralph had helped him get the processes organized with the larger team they had now, including the former Team 1, then gone off to work on something else they would need for tomorrow's volume production of cat trees. "Don't know what it is," he said, "but I think we're doing okay without him. Except for the mess we're making." He swung his meaty tattooed arm through an arc covering the work area. "Tools, planks, screws, scrap wood pieces, sandpaper…." He grimaced. "Sanding dust, dirty rags. You name it, we got it—everywhere." His gaze was somewhere in the distance as he said this. I waited. Something was coming.

He finally looked at me out of the corner of his eye and said hesitantly, "Would you mind if I put somebody on cleanup detail? With one less person actually working with tools part of the time, some tasks will be done slower, but I'm afraid we'll misplace something, or somebody will slip and fall, if we don't get better organized and get the trash out of the way."

I knew the answer to this one. I clapped him on the shoulder and said heartily, "Zeb, this is your team and your area. Keep it clean any way you want." Zeb thanked me and started checking his team members roster of skills to select the best cleanup person during prototype production. I went in search of Ellis, fingering Team 2's inspection procedures and considering how I was going to approach him.

He, Melissa, and Brad were still working together, close to the old Team 1 area by the driveway, making and attaching dangling cubes to platforms on the Team 3 prototype. I let them finish the cube they were working on. While I waited, I watched the game of tennis ball fetch across the street metamorphose into a new game. The tired dog went to where the kid had thrown the ball this time, picked it up in his mouth, and lay down, panting and grinning around the drool. He chewed on the ball, paying no attention to the kid's commands to come back. When the kid ran over and attempted to pry the ball from the Golden's jaws, the dog jumped up and led him a merry chase around the yard. The dog only needed to trot to keep ahead of the kid, so he was totally in control of this game. He finished with a flourish, drawing the kid through the spray from Dad's hose, then dropping the ball in a puddle and heading for the back yard. Dad fortunately wasn't upset; obviously this wasn't his first rodeo. He laughed, tousled his son's hair, and wiped his glasses with a dry portion of his T-shirt. He saw me watching, waved happily, and yelled something I couldn't hear. I waved back, then heard Ellis call my name, so I turned back to my version of reality.

"Thanks for waiting, Joe," he said. "What do you need?" I told him I was just reviewing things. I said they were doing a good job with the cubes—which they were—then attempted to ease into the inspection discussion. "Ellis, I was curious about the scratching post inspection. The task sequence—like when you checked squareness."

My ploy might have worked except for Melissa. "I told you!" she hissed. "We should have done it before the carpet!" At times teenagers don't exactly understand tact or diplomacy.

Ellis rolled with it, however. "Joe, it wasn't clear from your instructions when to check squareness. We made a judgment call to do it after the product was completed—in fact, we did all the inspections at that point. Seemed more efficient, and we were behind schedule after the issue with the rope winding." He shrugged. "It was a gamble, but a small one. And it paid off. We didn't find any errors that required correction. We had produced a good scratching post."

I shot Melissa a Don't Speak glance, perfected with our son and daughter as teenagers. "Okay, thanks." I didn't see any value in mentioning that you could make a squareness test come out any way you wanted if you used a carpenter's square on two joined carpeted surfaces—you could apply whatever pressure you needed on the carpet to make the attached surfaces appear to be square. You didn't have to be devious, just a believer in the quality of your work; we all have an almost infinite capacity to fool ourselves. The clincher was that I knew Ellis was correct in saying that my instructions weren't clear. I would have to develop standard inspection processes, using the intent and format of the Team 2 document.

Might as well do it now; as I mature I have learned to minimize putting things off. And everybody could use a break. I suggested to Ellis that they finish their current task, then take fifteen minutes. I snuck a quick peek at Melissa as I departed. Under her auburn and green hair was a wrinkled forehead evidencing her confusion about my behavior. I hoped she would figure it out when she saw my standard inspection procedures: being right should be adequate reward for her—there was no need to embarrass Ellis in public.

I mentioned the break to the other teams, synchronizing watches and agreeing when to restart the work. Then I went inside the house to ensure we had enough coffee, tea, and soft drinks. And prepare for a busy break time for myself. I had some serious computer work to do. I was sure several new cards lurked in my subconscious, waiting to be written. And I had to decide how far the teams were going to get today, so that we could finish up in a disciplined fashion instead of everybody simply wandering off at 4 PM. Too much to do, and too little time to do it in. *So what's new?*

***Setting An Example Is
Better Than Preaching***

SATURDAY ENDS—FINALLY

At my desk, wired to the gills, I punched up some serious rock-n-roll to accompany my word processing. Halfway through a driving piece reminiscent of early surf music, I realized that a fifteen minute break was hardly sufficient time to convert Team 2's impressive handwritten instructions into standard inspection procedures for cat climbing trees. I decided to do that task this evening. I settled now for adding a few thoughts to the **INSPECTION** card:

> Simple, standard inspection procedures & tools
> Point-of-production inspection
>   – minimize rework and delays
>   – correct process before future work is started

I considered the remainder of the afternoon, less than two hours—at least as people had been told. We could finish carpeting the climbing trees, assuming no further setbacks. The prototypes would be done, and I could finish revisions of the designs and production instructions. The only thing necessary was documentation—the teams already were aware of the revisions going forward to build the items in the quantities requested by the participants for their furry friends at home. I would also do the documentation this evening. A lot of evening work after a busy day. The needle on my internal stress-o-meter was swinging into the Caution zone.

Virginia stuck her lovely head around the door jamb to ask how things were going and then to tell me that Joe Junior's wife Rachel had called a few minutes ago. "She sounded worried, honey. I hope we haven't missed any signs from them that we should have picked up. She had to go before she could say much, but she said she would call back. Maybe I'll be able to get some idea before they come over."

The needle jumped from Caution to the Danger zone. I wasn't going to get a lot of sleep tonight, especially if Junior's visit demanded much time or attention from me. I expressed the hope that maybe Virginia could deal with them. "Wishful thinking, darling," she said kindly. I kissed her and headed back to the garage.

Striding through the kitchen, I noticed Ralph in the back yard, pacing the perimeter of the pool with his fingers under his chin in a pensive posture. What was he doing? I saw there were too many leaves floating on the water—maybe the automatic sweeper was on the fritz again. I would have to skim the surface with a net. *Mind definitely on Overload.*

Thirty seconds later, in the garage, I could see that the teams had beaten me back to work. Everybody was head down, serious on their tasks. Both remaining teams were getting ready to glue carpet onto their cat trees. Under Sandy's guidance Team 2 was obviously further along. *Good.* I hurried past them to Team 3 so that, before they got going, I could impart the knowledge about carpet attachment I had gained from my discussions with Ann and Ellis.

Zeb had no problem with Team 2's production sequence

for final assembly and carpet attachment, or their inspection steps, especially since Ellis, under the probing glare of Melissa, offered his support. But he did raise a valid point about staffing levels. "By completing final assembly first, we won't be able to utilize as many people for the carpeting. They would be falling all over each other if they all tried to work in the same confined space." I pursed my lips. He was right. How were we going to deal with this issue? Had Sandy and Mary thought of it?

My confusion was interrupted by a commotion in the Team 2 area. A team member named Mickey, accompanied by Ann and Mary, was woozily making his way across the floor to the driveway outside. Mickey, who lives three doors away, is an outstanding athlete at the high school. He looks like the offspring of a Marine colonel and an aerobics instructor, but his parents are both doctors, so he is smart as well as physically gifted. He carefully lowered himself to the driveway, halfway to the street, and I went over to see what was wrong. He looked up as I approached, and I could see his face was pale with dark circles forming under his eyes. He picked up on my concern and immediately reassured me.

"It's okay, Mr. Hall," he said as he breathed deeply. "This happens occasionally, as I told the team. Sometimes chemicals get to me. The glue was a little strong."

The rest of Team 2 had joined us. Ann said, "He was bothered a bit by the Team 1 glue, but they were at the outside end of the garage. We're far away from them." Which was true. I had chosen the end of the garage by the driveway for Team 1's location. They had the simplest product and least need for tools that were in cabinets at the inside end by the workbench. So, by coincidence they had the most fresh air and best ventilation. I nodded. Glue smells bothered me, too, but I hadn't thought they could be powerful enough to incapacitate someone. Paint and other strong petrochemicals, of course, are a different story: at the plant we take extensive precautions for protective equipment and adequate ventilation, and I have also learned to do so at home. I'm not taking chances with my family's health. And I didn't want to jeopardize Mickey's well-being. I pondered what to do.

"We missed this," Sandy said. "The product design and production process both have to be safe. And environmentally sound." I could see her mind whirring. "And throughout the life cycle of the product. The customer can't get sick or be injured." She looked me directly in the eye. "We can do this now. The team will update the design and process documentation. It won't jeopardize the schedule. Much."

"What do we do for right now?" I asked. "Put production on hold? And what do we do when you've finished the new design and process definitions? You'll need a different adhesive. Where will you get that?"

"Not a problem, sir," Mickey said, rising slowly to his feet. Color was returning to his cheeks. "We have some low-VOC non-toxic glue at home. I'll go get it. I'll be back in ten or fifteen minutes. It won't be enough for all the furniture, but it will get us through the prototypes. We can buy more later. I'll go to the store when we're done for today."

"I hate to be the wet blanket," said a slim woman in a blue running suit, "but do we have to go to all this trouble and expense? Can't we just assign the glueing work to people who aren't bothered by the smell?" It seemed like a sensible question to which I couldn't produce a rapid response.

Kim—the organized kid who had rewritten Team 2's instructions for the posts—spoke. "That's not entirely logical, Mrs. Jones. Everybody notices the smell of glue. Some people don't think the exposure bothers their performance, but it frequently does. Sometimes they only work slower. Other times they make mistakes—do lower quality work. I know I would rather work in fresh air than in contaminated air."

"So would I," Betty Jones retorted. "So would everybody. Should every work area be a 'clean room'? Where do you draw the line and be reasonable about it?" She was primed for combat, standing hands on hips with fire in her eyes.

"Nobody knows," Ralph said softly. I didn't realize he had rejoined the party. "Except the EPA, and frequently they are guessing. Every company has to make their own decisions about their own workers."

"This is the same discussion I sat in about paint fumes twenty years ago," I observed. "The directions of science and public policy are clear—fewer pollutants are better." I let my eyes swing around the group. "Besides, Mickey got sick, and I am not going to let that happen to anyone else here. This is not an abstract discussion. It's about everybody at my house today—including you, Betty. The work environment is going to be healthy." I pointed at Mickey. "Go get the safe glue, son. We'll do something else until you get back." He thanked me and started down the sidewalk towards his house.

"Ralph and I have an idea about what to do," Zeb said. "Not many people are needed for carpeting. They can do dry runs of the carpeting tasks—cutting, transport, placement— minimizing flow and wait times—developing efficient motions. By the time they're done with that, Mickey will have returned with his adhesive, so they will perform the actual carpeting in their team areas. The people not needed for carpeting will go with Ralph now. He wants to get started on some of the tasks for volume production tomorrow."

News to me. I glanced questioningly at Ralph who was fiddling with his shirt buttons, obviously discomfited by Zeb's announcement of his intentions. Sandy was amused. Ralph is normally Mr. Tact who would never blind-side someone with a new thought before discussing it with them.

"It is a possibility that Zeb and I discussed," Ralph said, "with the purpose of bringing it to everyone's attention if it made sense. Zeb had observed that not everybody would be needed for the carpeting activities, and I was considering the production processes that would be needed for the production of the furniture models in volumes higher than the single model each of the prototypes." *Nice introduction.* He went on to say that he had a preliminary plan for layout of the production process in the back yard, and that he wanted to explore its feasibility. He thought it would be useful to construct a few main subassemblies, such as platforms, in back yard locations that would approximate a smooth production flow. He and the workers would test, and then revise, the production flow for the various models of furniture. "In conjunction with the prototype processes confirmed in the garage this afternoon, we would have the capability to produce the required models and quantities tomorrow."

I expected to see the willow tree do somersaults or a flying saucer land on the front lawn. The world had gone nuts. "You're thinking of building subassemblies in batches?" I asked in disbelief. *On the shelf project, I insisted on batch building of subassemblies. The new Joe was incredulous at the concept.*

He shook his head. "No. We'll build items as required—keep inventory low. But we will have designated locations for effective production of each item—including short transit time to its using location."

"Got it." I shouldn't have worried. I thanked Ralph for his ideas, then two groups formed: one to dry run carpeting processes with Teams 2 and 3, which had not yet started carpeting, the other to work with Ralph and Zeb on production processes after the prototyping.

Mickey soon returned with two quart cans of adhesive that would see us through the prototypes. He had also brought fresh squeeze-bottle applicators. The carpeters started working for real. I debated whether to join them or the back yard process group, then decided I would instead focus on improving my stress-o-meter readings. I returned to my office to see if I could make any progress on generating standard inspection procedures.

Forty minutes later, I had successfully supplemented, revised, and cut-and-pasted inspection procedures, then incorporated them by reference into the manufacturing instructions. Out my office window overlooking the private back yard with its perimeter of silver maple and ash trees, I watched Ralph patiently working with people on the production processes and flow. I briefly wondered how he was going to bring the carpeters up to speed, then realized he didn't have to—their jobs wouldn't change, since the carpeting took place after final assembly, and they had already worked out efficient processes for themselves.

While my keyboard rested, my mind moseyed over to the issue of product design, particularly how I had missed so many things. Clearly I had not employed a design process that unerringly generated quality designs. I knew I was fortunate that major design errors hadn't manifested themselves. I was ruminating about both my good luck and how the design process might be improved if I ever had to do this again, when Sandy reappeared to tell me that everybody thought they were done for the day. The two remaining prototypes had been built and inspected. People had been able to devote some time to the volume production processes, and Ralph was satisfied with the progress there. This was the best news about the project since the first five minutes of it! I followed Sandy to the garage.

The teams were anxious for my review and approval. Over the next twenty minutes, I ascertained that the climbing tree prototypes had indeed been properly constructed. Minimal final inspections and no rework had been required as a result of Sandy's use of interim inspection points, added to the INSPECTION STATUS board. With the scratching post, the cat trees represented successful output from our first day. Although Ralph said that a few kinks remained to be resolved, he was pleased with the progress on process design for higher volume production. Proof of the progress was present to a degree in the form of some platform subassemblies and center posts in the back yard, a few of them partially assembled.

We were actually done 300 seconds before 4 PM! I congratulated everybody and said I was looking forward to continuing tomorrow morning at 10 (Sandy and Ralph earlier). Most of the group waved and walked away, some to their cars and some to the sidewalk. Luis from Team 3 asked if he could back his SUV into the driveway to load his cat tree. I was digesting his unexpected comment when Mary asked the same thing about Team 2's tree. Ellis completed the hat trick of flummoxing me when he said he would just put his scratching post under his arm and walk home with it. And proceeded to do so.

My Lord! People thought they could take the prototypes home today! The possibility had never occurred to me. I had planned to spend time this evening going over the prototypes to pick up lessons I had missed during the day. Given Ellis's precedent, that was clearly going to be impossible. I mumbled a stunned

"Sure" to Luis and Mary, then stood motionless as a stone statue while they backed their vehicles into the driveway, moving out of the way only when Sandy took my arm and dragged me onto the lawn.

I finally popped out of my catatonic state and helped load the cat trees into the vehicles. Or started to do so, until both Mary and Luis expressed concerns that the pointed corners of the platforms and base, even though they were carpeted, might scrape their vehicle's interior and leave marks. Several torn-up old sheets and towels for padding solved the problem.

"A new issue," Sandy remarked. "Post-production packaging and product protection. We can cut up used cardboard boxes to make corner protectors for the cat trees. Easier and cheaper than looting your closets for old sheets and towels." Her comment brought to mind the occasional problems we had at the plant with customer complaints of damaged merchandise. I didn't really know how we were defining and implementing packaging requirements for customer shipments. Something else to look into on Monday.

After everybody had departed, Virginia asked when I wanted dinner. With tasks to complete before I could allow my mind to shift out of work gear, I told her "in an hour or two." I went to my office and finished the documentation. I also wrote down everything I could remember about the prototypes—since I didn't have them to look at. When my subconscious mind started popping up questions later, I wanted to have some notes to refer to.

Dinner was braised monkfish, pasta primavera, and a mixed greens salad (pasta and salad for us; Buzzy prefers his fish solo). Virginia said that Rachel had called again, deferring her and Junior's visit until tomorrow evening. "She didn't sound like herself, sweetheart. There's something going on." So, naturally, we worried about them for the rest of the meal, imagining dire and not-so-dire circumstances in their lives.

After dinner, we knew we had to relax, getting Junior and the cat furniture off our minds for a little while. We went straight to our 'media center'—two recliners in front of the TV in the family room, set side by side so we can hold hands while Buzzy takes turns between our laps. We watched a movie that had enough action to command our attention. Then Virginia went on to bed to read until I got there, while I did the last thing I knew I had to do today on the cat furniture project. I transcribed my note cards into the red spiral-bound journal I had created either last Wednesday or three years ago—it seemed like eons since the project had started.

Before I turned off the computer, I checked email one last time. The only Inbox messages were from a couple of neighbors who had been present at today's adventure in production. I didn't read them—either a very smart or a very dumb thing to do. I joined Virginia in bed and replied "Fine. In fact, excellent." when she asked how the day had gone. Which was true, all things considered. I summarized the day's activities, culminating with prototypes going home with their owners. We both smiled, tired but happy. Ignorance is bliss.

A Shortcut Seldom Is

***Rather Light A Candle Than
Complain About The Darkness***

ANOTHER ROCKY MORNING

I dreamed about cats. Not surprising, since my life at the moment consisted of designing and constructing cat furniture. Only my dreams featured big cats—jaguars, leopards, cougars, lions, and a couple of black panthers. They were napping, jumping, and generally romping around on colossal cat trees that made the ones we were building seem like doll house furniture. The fearsome felines were enjoying themselves, paying scant attention to me. Until suddenly all motion ceased, furry heads swivelled towards me, and a dozen pairs of green and yellow eyes fixed on me as though I were breakfast.

Startled, I woke up. Looked around the bedroom—no foreign entities. My heart rate subsided. Nice to know that my subconscious mind could recognize a survival situation and get out of it. Perhaps an omen that the day would go well; I am the perpetual optimist.

The clock displayed 6:18 AM. No point in trying to get back to sleep, so I slid out of bed very quietly. Shaved and made coffee. Buzzy was absent, not cruising around my ankles as a sinuous mobile obstacle course. Odd—but then cats follow their own bliss. When they start becoming predictable, they get a stern lecture from the Cat Behavior Police and are put on probation. If they don't return to proper feline deportment, their reservoir of remaining lives is decremented one from whatever they have left from their original nine.

I walked down the tiled hallway into my office to check email and plan the day. Buzzy was sleeping in the green leather chair facing my desk. Okay. Now I knew where he was. I logged in to find 93 emails—par for weekend overnight.

My spam filter had identified 77 emails. A quick review verified they were junk. Of the remaining 16 emails, I printed out 9 from neighbors who had worked on the cat furniture yesterday, or whose family members had.

The emails came in three flavors, exemplified by those from Ellis, Mickey's mother, and Kim's father:

From: Ellis
To: Joe Hall
Sent: Sunday, 6:03 AM
Subject: Congratulations!

Just letting you know that our cats are enjoying their scratching post. I enjoyed working on it yesterday (much more fun than building shelves). Looking forward to another great day!

Ellis

From: Doctor Deborah
To: Joe Hall
Sent: Saturday, 8:59 PM
Subject: Mickey - Thanks!

Dear Joe,
Thanks so much for taking action on Mickey's allergies and substituting the non-toxic low-VOC glue. Tom and I are pleased to know somebody is taking consumers' health seriously. I assume you are also taking into

account flammability and other concerns of the Consumer Product Safety Commission. There is a great volume of statutes and regulations regarding consumer products, and we want to assure you of our gratitude for not only following them, but going beyond them with materials that are safe for sensitive individuals like our son.

Debbie

From: Mark N.
To: Joe Hall
Sent: Saturday, 9:19 PM
Subject: Cat furniture project

Mr. Hall,
We wish to thank you for your understanding today. As you know, Kim is very detail-oriented. We are grateful for your thoughtfulness and ability to use Kim's talents successfully on the cat furniture project.

At our home this evening, we discussed the attributes of the cat furniture being constructed by your work teams. We would like to know what you envision for the longevity of the product, that is, how many years of use you anticipate receiving from the furniture. Although we are paying only a small amount for our scratching post and climbing tree, we would like to be assured that they will have useful lives equivalent to or better than commercially available merchandise.

Thank you.

Mark

Virginia was in the kitchen when I went for more coffee. I munched a day-old cheese Danish and she had a slice of cinnamon coffee cake. "This is moderation, dear," she said. "One for each of us." I didn't say anything.

I showed her the 9 emails from project people. She read them and said, "So the good news is, people love your product.

And the way you're building it—the new Joe. The bad news is, they want to be sure it won't stain, fall apart, or otherwise have problems over its lifetime. A long lifetime. And they want to turn your ad-hoc back yard operation into a full-blown factory turning out federally-approved and state-approved products. All of which you can't really blame them for. You said you could build cat furniture that was as good as the pet store stuff. Or better."

"Yeah," I said, "I did. It promises to be an interesting day. The new Joe feels like the proverbial duck paddling like heck under the water while maintaining a calm outward appearance. And now he has lead weights hanging from his webbed feet."

"You'll get through it," she said. "You always do. Somehow."

"I hope so," I said. Hope was the key word there. I swallowed my last bit of cheese Danish, noting idly that Buzzy had not made an appearance. Odd—he loves cream cheese. But that thought didn't last long. I went into the garage to consider my predicament.

And that is where this tale started, with me trying to figure out *What Do I Do Now?* The project had looked fine last night, but was now lurching towards an out-of-control condition with expanding customer requirements and additional production considerations. I went back into the house to get a pad and pen to make notes. I was going to be prepared for action by the time my guests arrived at ten o'clock.

My first note said *what the heck do the feds want?* With a Jimmy Buffett CD in the background, I logged onto the Consumer Product Safety Commission (CPSC) website. Waded through legalese on 'Standards for Surface Flammability" and other similar topics. Learned I was dealing with two issues: safety of components of the cat furniture, such as carpet coverings; and safety of the assembled unit itself. Learned that there were both mandatory and voluntary standards for certain products. Also discovered that potentially there were state regulations to deal with.

And so on through many brain-numbing Web hyperlinks. I stayed fresh with coffee, deep breathing, and a little stretching (a little is all I can do). Walked briefly around the back yard which needed mowing—although it probably wouldn't after it had been a factory-for-a-day today.

Fast forward one and a half hours. Good news and bad news. Good news was that the cat furniture was almost certainly legal if the components I bought met their applicable statutes and regulations—and they had to meet them in order to be sold in the U.S. I sent emails to CPSC departments and state agencies to verify my conclusion; within a few days I would have documentation that the scratching posts and climbing trees met all voluntary and mandatory guidelines.

Bad news was that I knew I had scampered through a rainstorm without getting wet. There could easily have been legal requirements that would have sunk me. I was going to have to do something about this continuing problem of needing to revise designs because of new requirements from customers—or, in this case, relevant third parties such as the Consumer Product Safety Commission.

Thinking of potential third party influences gave me a jolt. I hurriedly checked the web sites of ASTM, ANSI, and other standards-setting organizations for materials, processes, and products. I found out that they weren't interested in pet furniture—no big surprise, but I still felt relieved. And more helpless than ever, since I hadn't even considered these groups until a couple of minutes ago. Jimmy was singing about how the mess down in Margaritaville was possibly all his own fault. I could relate. I had to get more organized.

Virginia stepped into my office to say she was going to make a breakfast run for us and for our guests. "Frankly, sweetheart, you look like you could use a triple-shot latte. I'll get a couple for you. Non-fat." I assured her that one would be sufficient. She waved and departed with good wishes for my efforts. "Good luck in figuring out how to keep everybody happy with their cat trees for as long as they have them."

It was the second time this morning Virginia had mentioned the lifetime of the cat trees. Maybe she knew something I didn't. I traded Jimmy Buffet for the radio and simply sat for a while, thinking deeply as the sun crept up the sky on the right side of the back yard. The realization eventually came to me that the product life cycle was the key. I had to consider customer and third party requirements over the product's entire life cycle from birth until death (either upgrade or environmentally safe disposal). That was the only way to prevent unanticipated design revisions—at least ones that could have been known at the time.

By the time my wife returned struggling with drinks and grocery bags, I had jotted down categories of information to know about our product's life cycle—functionality (what it did under what conditions); cost (purchase, lifetime); physical attributes (size, weight, stability); appearance & aesthetics; materials; surface treatments (coverings, finishes, coatings); transport & storage; use & operation; safety; environmental impact; reliability; longevity; care & maintenance; and so on through the product's eventual demise. I checked the list against neighbors' emails and was pleased I hadn't missed anything. I could take care of Kim's father's product longevity issue and concerns of people who were worried in various ways about the product's performance and taking care of it throughout its lifetime.

Virginia's purchases were on the kitchen counter: fruit, yogurt, three types of bagels, low-fat cream cheese. "Where's the good stuff?" I asked. "Doughnuts and Danishes?"

"Not today," she said brightly. "I'll toast blueberry bagels for us." While she did so, I explained what I had done. "So I wrote down things like, 'cat tree should last ten years in normal use,' and 'cat tree should be easy to clean.' My problem now is how to get design specifications and designs from those requirements. Which are clear to customers, but somewhat vague to product designers."

We discussed the issue while we polished off breakfast—the low-fat cream cheese actually wasn't bad—and watched a pair of robins hop around the back yard, one of them successfully pulling a squirming meal from the lawn. A quartet of sparrows fluttered around the ski chalet bird feeder. On the wood slat fence sat a couple of magpies, considering whether to harass one of the other species. Another magpie couple dropped in for a conversation, and shortly the four took off, probably to locate an unfortunate squirrel to annoy.

We broke down the requirements into specifics. The basic structure should hold together firmly for ten years. The carpet covering was a major issue. Its wearability under cat abuse should be a minimum of five years. It should be cleanable of cat stains using non-toxic household cleaning products, with no more difficulty than cleaning a normal human-induced spot on a carpet. And so forth for many pages. With my loved one's help, I had a set of reasonable design specifications.

But I now had another problem. Did my designs satisfy the specifications? No problem with the structure. However, I clearly did not know enough about the characteristics of the carpet I had purchased. For instance, everybody has seen advertisements for cleaning coffee or wine spills from carpet—advertisements for either carpet brands or cleaning products. Our cat doesn't drink wine or coffee, and I doubt that many cats do. They have different problems, ones that need to be taken care of with cleaning products that are not toxic to cats and do not leave harmful residues.

"I need another latte," I said as I stood up. "I'll get it while I'm out." *Full fat.* I needed to visit Karpet Klatch where I had purchased the carpet, to check out information on it—care, durability, warranty, Material Safety Data Sheets, and so on. Virginia said she would make sure Sandy and Ralph got enough caffeine and food if they arrived before I returned. She started getting out paper plates, plastic utensils and glasses, napkins, and taking them to the round patio table. I left on my mission.

Long story short, I returned from my expedition with a stack of catalog sheets and other papers in the front passenger seat and a pile of carpet pieces in the back seat—different carpet maker and brand than previously. This new carpet would meet the specs. I had also purchased inexpensive aluminum stands for the INSPECTION STATUS boards for each team. Ralph and Sandy were in the kitchen with plates bearing only crumbs in front of them. I popped the lid off my latte and explained what had happened while I drank it.

"Okay, so no real harm done," Sandy said. "The structural designs are sound. The carpet covering has changed. And the adhesive. But you bought both of those." Which I had, seeing no reason to burden Mickey with being the adhesive supplier.

"You were lucky," Ralph said matter-of-factly. "You could have ended up redesigning the entire product, now that you finally have all the requirements and specs defined."

"Sure was," I agreed. "I have a new appreciation for the role of design in producing a quality product." *And, on Monday morning, a lot of work for some surprised product planners and engineers at the plant. Big changes are coming!*

The three of us talked about the upcoming day. Ralph had put in a couple of hours at home last night, estimating build times for the components of cat scratching posts and cat trees. "Creating a planning framework for the production," he said.

Sandy had reviewed the process documentation, including inspection. "It's good," she said, "except for the changes to the carpet and adhesive. Maybe you also need different cutting tools for the carpet—I don't know anything about the new carpet you bought."

"Got that covered," I said. But I did need to document it. I left them to continue planning the day's production and hurried to my office. I wasn't sure whether I needed music to keep myself wired or to calm down. I opted for the latter and made the revisions to the designs and the manufacturing instructions. I changed all the imbedded information to references—the carpet, adhesive, and tools—so that future updates if necessary could be made easily to the referenced information while keeping the basic documentation intact. The cut-and-paste feature of PC word processors is one of the key unsung inventions of the 20th Century.

A sad song about an inattentive lover reminded me that I needed to record my insights about design requirements and specifications. I created two new index cards.

PRODUCT REQUIREMENTS

Include customer and relevant third parties
- third parties are government, consumer groups, standards organizations, professional societies, etc.

Cover entire life cycle of product

Document as clearly and quantitatively as possible
- includes criteria for knowing if requirements are met

DESIGN FOR REQUIREMENTS

Translate product requirements into design specifications
- specs must be unambiguous
- must be clear link from requirement to spec

Designs then are created to meet specifications
- must know how to measure spec compliance
- must document that designs satisfy specifications

Finished, I was musing about the innumerable elements of creating quality when Virginia called from the front door. "Joe, Zeb is here. Says he knows he is early, but he wanted to talk to you." I put the philosophical issues of quality out of my mind and went to see what had gotten the big man out of bed a half hour earlier than necessary.

Zeb accepted a bagel with a mound of butter, then led me to the Team 3 area in the garage, which had the biggest variety of materials and therefore contained the lion's share of the mess of wood scraps, carpet remnants, and loose fasteners. He admitted his cleanup plan had failed.

"I thought about it last night," he said, licking his fingers and stroking his curly red beard in a contemplative fashion. "All I can figure out is that people kept trashing their areas after Betty cleaned up because they weren't accountable—Betty was.

Today I'm going to assign people to keep their own work zones clean. We'll see if that works better."

After Zeb received my approval for the change in cleanup approach, he grabbed a push broom and waste box and went to work. I told him he didn't have to do that, but he said that the mess happened on his watch and continued sweeping. I went back to the kitchen to refill my coffee mug and synchronize my plans for the day with Ralph's and Sandy's.

By ten minutes before ten o'clock I was back in the now-pristine garage (Zeb had magnanimously cleaned up the small messes in the Team 1 and 2 areas as well as the Team 3 area), waiting for the first Sunday workers to arrive. Zeb was with Sandy and Ralph in the back yard, where today's production would take place since we would need much more space than was necessary for building the prototypes. The weather was cooperating with our plans. The light blue morning sky had few clouds, and a gentle breeze rippled the irises and the black locust tree displaying its pink blooms beside the yellow-green adornment of the weeping willow. Frequently the efforts of human beings seem insignificant in comparison to nature.

Within a few minutes the street curbs began to fill up with sedans, coupes, pickup trucks, and SUVs. *Ladies and gentlemen, please make sure your tray tables are stowed and your seat backs are in the upright and locked position. Fasten your seat belts low and tight across your middle. We are ready for takeoff.* I inhaled deeply and tried to prepare myself for today's entertainment at Joe's Cat Carnival.

***The Moon Is Not Moved
When The Wind Blows***

NEW ISSUES TO DEAL WITH

Everybody was jovial, anticipating another successful day, helping themselves to the drinks and goodies set up on the patio table. I schmoozed with everybody while my stomach growled, missing its sugary fried dough. Then I rolled into my group moderator's role, distributing and describing production drawings and instructions for today's cat furniture output.

At my request, Ralph and Sandy stepped forward and explained the production flow. Sandy spoke first. "Same basic approach as yesterday with three work areas set up by type of scratching post or cat tree, just with more models and a few more work teams. The higher-volume models will be produced more or less continually by dedicated teams, the lower-volume models by teams that switch among models. Different skills, training, and tool requirements, obviously—described in the paper Joe passed out. We think we have things under control." She smiled and sipped her coffee. "Of course, reality will prove that we missed something, but we will have a solid framework within which to react."

As a refresher, Ralph summarized production processes: materials operations (such as carpet cutting); subassembly (platforms, condos, danglies) including carpeting; subassembly inspection (in-process and finished); final assembly; final inspection. "The only big change today is to carpet portions of subassemblies when building them. Smoother production flow and shorter cycle times are achieved that way."

After asking for process questions and receiving none, he continued. "As Joe mentioned, we estimated cycle times for activities. We used those to develop a build sequence for the scratching posts and climbing trees that keeps the work load balanced through the day. Since units vary in work content, we sequenced production of different models in order to maintain an overall level work content—as much as possible. As Sandy said, we will react when the need arises." He asked for questions again. Nobody said anything, although a few faces wore expressions indicating possible confusion over his last statement. *React to what? React how?* I guess they figured they would see how the system worked instead of asking questions now. I was sorry they hadn't asked. I would have liked to hear the answers, since I didn't exactly get that part myself. I hoped my ignorance wouldn't come back to bite me.

Ralph distributed a build schedule. On my copy I saw that the plan was for each final assembly team to turn out a finished cat tree approximately every 45 minutes on average, in less time for scratching posts. That rate would get us the required production easily, with time in the day to spare. I didn't know if the intent was to finish early, or if he and Sandy were planning for contingencies. I supposed that either goal was okay—either way people would leave no later than they had planned, presumably happy with the new furniture for their furry friends at home.

To the accompaniment of ebullient gestures and cries of "Let's do it!" people collected coffee, tea, and water and moved towards their work areas. I was about to go inside and tell

Virginia the day had kicked off well, when I saw a lanky fellow heading towards me.

The guy was tall with close-cropped gray-brown hair. He wore pressed slacks, a blue chambray shirt, and sported silvered sunglasses. He looked like a highway patrolman. He also looked like he meant business.

"Good morning, Avery," I greeted him with a warm hand-shake. I have known Avery for about ten years; he works for a local manufacturer of mobile home accessories. His teenage son Carson had planned to work on the project, but had dropped out because of a conflict with a school event. I wondered what had prompted Avery to come by.

"Hi, Joe," he said, pumping my hand firmly. "Ellis called and told me about yesterday. Sounded like fun, so I thought I would join in today. That okay with you?"

"The more the merrier," I said cheerfully. *Be a good test of our documents and training.*

"Good. I thought you'd say that. You're a good guy, Joe. There's something else, too." *There usually is.* Sipping coffee, keeping a neutral expression, I asked what.

Avery explained that they really needed the cat tree Carson had planned to make—"just can't afford the store stuff, Joe." However, they wanted their tree to be somewhat different: mixed carpet colors and mixed platform sizes. The carpet was easy, since I had purchased some new colors this morning. A variety of platform sizes for a single cat tree was, of course, a totally different matter. I was considering how to respond when Kim joined our little gathering and asked, "Mr. Hall, my dad wondered if we could have our cat tree with one more platform. He wants our cats to get more jumping exercise." *Oh, this is wonderful. Like real customers at the plant—last minute design changes.* At the plant we would quote delivery delays and price increases for the change orders. Somehow I knew that wasn't an acceptable response in my current situation. Unfortunately, I had no clue as to the correct reply.

I was saved by the sound of the sliding glass door from the house. Virginia came up to me with a tense expression. "Joe, I need to see you inside. Right now." I hastily called Ralph up to deal with Avery and Kim, then gratefully (I hoped, not knowing what issue lurked inside the house) exited the patio.

"It's Buzzy," she said. "He can't move his rear legs." We went into my office. Buzzy was lying on the floor with a plate of cat treats and his favorite canned food in front of him. They were untouched. When he saw us, he attempted to stand up and failed, his rear legs collapsing beneath him.

"Of course," I said. "It's Sunday." A law of nature—pets get seriously injured or ill only on days or at times that our usual veterinarian's office is closed.

"Right," she said. "You get the cat carrier, I'll get a towel and a bowl of water. We're going to visit the Emergency Veterinary Clinic again." The emergency clinic is a marvelous institution to have available at nights and on weekends. Very good doctors work there. For a very good price, of course; we were looking at a minimum hundred dollar price tag. No choice, though. I went to get the cat carrier—basically a small cage with a handle.

Over many years and cats we have mastered this drill. Rapid action, minimal panic despite emotions going bonkers. In twenty minutes Virginia was backing out of the driveway with Buzzy. I returned to my earlier problem in the back yard.

Ralph and company had departed the patio, but Sandy was sitting in one of the padded white wrought iron chairs. I told her about Buzzy and she expressed sympathy. Her Persian cat is ageing, too.

Then: "Team 2 has a problem." *Why not? Why should I have expected today to be any different than yesterday?* I walked with Sandy to Mary and Ann standing beside two small piles of parts.

Mary was still leading Team 2. "These brackets are defective. The plating is spotty." I nodded. The plating defects were pinpricks, but the brackets would be susceptible to corrosion. Ann said, "These screws have funny stuff on the heads. I think Sandy called them burrs?" Right again.

I decided to deal with the screws first. "The screws come in boxes of 100. We have plenty in the garage. We'll bring out boxes of screws and work from bulk stock instead of having precisely the right number at subassembly and assembly."

"You think it's a good idea for production people to spend time sorting through screws to find good ones they can use?" Sandy asked. *Good point.*

"We can sort off-line," I said. "Off the critical path. Keep production moving."

"Using who?" Ann said. "We don't have any spare people." *At the plant we do. That's their jobs—sort out defective material, document it, return it to the supplier with the supporting paperwork, then follow up for the credit. Is something wrong with this picture?*

"It's temporary," Sandy said. "I'll do it." She rapidly fingered through the pile of screws. "Here are twenty good ones. Start with these while I find more." Ann left to resume work.

"How about brackets?" Mary asked. "You have extra brackets?" I shook my head No; I had purchased the right quantity for prototypes and today's production.

With the team we discussed what to do. There was a suggestion to use the poorly-plated brackets, anyway, because the defects were tiny and they would be out of sight under a layer of carpet. Fortunately, that notion was quickly killed. Quality is throughout a product, not only on the surface.

The team needed to get back to work, so I followed Sandy's example. I located enough good brackets to jump-start their production, then while they restarted work I went to the garage and hand-sorted out the remaining good ones. I gave those to Mary, then drove to the home improvement store to hand select enough more good ones for today's production.

The department manager wasn't happy to see me tearing open plastic bags of brackets and discarding defective ones. She called over the store manager, who said, "Those defects are minor and they're allowable. Our corporate staff negotiates an acceptable quality level with the supplier; they have to produce 98% good brackets, and that's good enough for us."

"Two questions," I said. "If that's true, why do I have more than 2% bad brackets here?"

"The 98% is over their entire production run. Obviously any store can get some batches with more defects."

"Obviously," I said. "Second question. What's their annual bracket production volume? Hundreds of thousands? On every hundred thousand brackets, your stores want to stick the consumer with two thousand bad ones. Customers should buy more than they need so they can sort out and discard the bad ones? Not for me, thanks." I resumed tearing and sorting.

When I got home, I put the good brackets in the garage, then sat at the kitchen counter with a big cup of hot juice from the bean of the Coffea Arabica plant. I prepared an index card reflecting the experience with brackets and screws:

MATERIALS QUALITY

Make sure production receives only good parts/material
- inspect and sort before production if necessary
- safety stock if required to keep production going

Better solution is to purchase only good parts/material
- supplier (maker, distributor, etc.) inspects, sorts

Best solution is maker produces only good parts/material
- i.e., maker has effective quality systems

Satisfied (for now—the card might be expanded later), I put the card into my pocket and went out to see what was happening in what Virginia had called my back yard factory.

Team 2 was roaring along in full production. A scratching post was almost finished in the Team 1 area, and Team 3 also seemed busy. It looked like Zeb had already put Avery to work under Betty's guidance. Avery was working with military thoroughness, consulting instruction sheets frequently, and I assumed the scheduled times for his output had been adjusted for his levels of skills and training. And would be adjusted again as he gained speed.

Ellis waved me over to the Team 1 area in front of the dwarf pussy willow tree. The tree's light brown branches were dotted with still-closed green buds and opened small gray blobs of fuzz. It was an idyllic scene, but I didn't imagine Ellis wanted to congratulate me on our landscaping.

"Hi, Joe," Ellis said. "We're doing pretty well here. Got the quality issues with the screws and winding rope under control. Ran into something at final inspection, though." He showed me the seams of the carpet surrounding the post below the rope section. They were uneven—not terribly so, but evidently the quality bug had bitten Team 1. *Good.*

"It's not the attaching or fastening, or whatever you call it," Melissa said. "The edges of the carpet aren't straight." I peered closely. She was right.

"I don't know if the carpet knife got dull, or if you're stronger than we are and were able to cut yesterday's pieces straight," Ellis said. "But we've got a problem."

Probably a little bit of both. But the carpet knife certainly wasn't sharp enough. I sharpened it in the garage and tested it slicing a page of a newspaper from the recycle bin (not a scientific test that would be acceptable at the plant, but fine for carpet cutting). I gave the knife back to Team 1, but I knew the issue of quality tools was lying in the weeds for all the teams. They probably had some screwdrivers that had been used too many times as chisels and some pliers with loose or worn jaws. I had to do something proactive and not simply wait until a problem arose. I was trying to think of a solution when Mary and Sandy walked up. I am no longer bashful about asking for advice, so I did so. "The problem, of course, is more than taking bad tools out of service. Tools need to be checked periodically to be sure they are still sharp, or straight, or whatever."

Mary was stumped, but Sandy (bless her organized soul) had an idea. "Joe, do you have any colored stickers of any kind? For file folders or bulk mail, or anything?" I told her Virginia had sheets of various-sized colored shapes—dots, squares, etc.—with adhesive backing. She used them for crafts.

"Use those," Sandy said. "Certify the tools, then apply colored dots to the tool handle, or wherever. Red means re-certification every 30 days, blue every 60 days, and so on. Or a different code—maybe the color is the month for re-certification, or the quarter. Doesn't matter what the code is as long as people can tell if a tool certification is valid for current use."

It was brilliant. And it would work at the plant, too. There we had formal tool inspection procedures with scheduled maintenance by tool serial number or groups of like tools, but the system was too cumbersome for widespread application. Things like small hand tools and stepladders didn't get certified and inevitably caused production defects or injuries. This idea would be a useful supplement.

I thanked her and turned to leave, to ask Luis and Ellis to take on the task of certifying tools, but Mary and Sandy each grabbed an arm and reminded me that they actually had come to ask me for something. They stepped me into the kitchen.

"You picked our brains for free," Sandy said. "Now you owe us something." I asked them what.

"You gave us printed copies of the updated requirements you prepared. From the CPSC and so on. Remember?" I did.

"Could you copy the files to a CD?" Mary asked. "Now?" "Or," she amended, "at least soon?"

A dilemma. If I asked why they wanted the CD, it would appear that I was questioning their judgment or micro-managing unnecessarily. And I would almost certainly make the CD, anyway. So I just said "Sure" and asked if I could take care of the tools issue first. No problem, they said, and I went to find Luis and Ellis, wondering if I actually should have done more probing regarding the CD. Sometimes you can't win.

A Sharp Knife Has Many Uses;
A Dull One, None

ARE WE MAKING PROGRESS?

I copied the requirements files, gave the CD to Mary, and sat at the kitchen counter with fresh coffee and green grapes, picking one at a time off the bunch, wanting a Danish. Virginia's favorite radio station was playing softly. I am not totally comfortable with classical music, but sometimes it is quite soothing. The names of composers, conductors, and the pieces themselves will always be beyond me. Although I knew I had heard it before, I couldn't have named the violin selection playing at the moment to win season passes to my favorite football team. I updated one of my cards to read:

QUALITY - RESOURCES

Align resource capabilities with tasks to be done
- verified/certified capabilities

Make sure equipment and tools don't cause problems
- conduct preventive maintenance (PM) program
- periodically inspect and re-certify non-PM items
- make sure people understand routine care

I took the opportunity to flip through all the note cards in my pocket to see if any other ones needed to be revised. They seemed okay, and I was pleased to see that there were several good concepts on the cards. Refreshed and calm, with the violin melody playing in my head, I went back outside.

There was a commotion going on in the Team 3 area. Apparently today's episode of the Roger and Zeb show—little Roger was pointing up at big Zeb like a mountain climber showing the location of the summit. His voice was loud, although not as angry as yesterday.

"I was trying to make my schedule! What am I supposed to do, let work stack up unfinished?" Looking down at Roger, Zeb too showed less emotion than before. Guess they were getting used to each other. "What's the problem, guys?" I said.

Roger had been assigned relatively simple tasks, including subassembly of dangling toys for cat trees—fuzzy balls and the like with attached cords. In final assembly the cords were fastened to the underside of platforms, so they hung down for cats to play with. Luis, the final assembly person, wasn't pleased with Roger's work. The toy hung down too far.

"I'm supposed to be able to staple the last quarter inch of the cord to the platform's underside," Luis said. "I shouldn't have to measure to check that the cord is the correct length for this platform on this cat tree. The toy should come to me with the cord cut to the correct length."

"What's the big deal?" Roger asked. "Just whack off the extra inch. Or whatever. I got it to you on time." I could see that he was genuinely puzzled.

"I don't have scissors or a knife," Luis said patiently. "Yes, I could find one quickly, but it's not my job. Fixing your mistakes would just put me behind."

"How did it pass inspection?" I asked. Seemed like a reasonable question.

"It's my fault," Betty said almost inaudibly. "Roger told me it had to go to Luis to make schedule, and I had other inspections to do. It looked okay, so I sent it on."

"What in the heck—" I began, then clamped shut my lips. *I am not behaving that way anymore. There is a new Joe.* "All right," I said calmly. "Let's figure out what happened and prevent future occurrences. We need everybody to do their jobs on time, but also to do them completely and correctly." Roger started to object, but Melissa said stonily, "Just chill, okay?"

"Nobody's blaming you, Roger," I said. "Let's just see how to make things better." I noticed that Sandy and Ralph had drifted over and were watching this new person in Joe's body with some amusement. With both Team 2 and 3 participating, we reviewed Roger's subassembly process in detail. Measuring and cutting lengths of cord wasn't difficult, but it was clear that mistakes could happen. Ralph suggested a template—basically a straightedge—for the correct cord length. "Perhaps with a cutting edge on the end. Simply stretch the cord to the correct length on the template and cut it by pulling it over the end."

"I'll go you one better," Sandy said. "Ideally you want to cut the cord to length after it is attached to the toy. Make a V-notch in the non-cutting end of the template. Pull the cord through it until the toy lodges securely in the notch, then cut it to length on the cutting end." She looked pleased with herself. I wasn't surprised; Sandy has always been an excellent Manufacturing Engineer. "Color code the templates," she added. "So the right one is used for each different length. The manufacturing instruction would be a graphic illustration of how to perform the operation, showing the color. Foolproof."

"It wouldn't need to be inspected then, would it?" asked Betty. "My workload would go down. And the time in the schedule for inspection wouldn't be needed."

"My task would be easier, too," Roger said. "Takes a whole lot less time to pull a cord over a cutting edge than to measure, mark, and cut."

Everybody nodded. Bright lights appeared in the eyes of people who were eager to apply Sandy's concept to their processes. That was fine with me. If something wasn't done to increase production efficiency, we weren't going to get all the scratching posts and cat trees built today, since the problems in all work teams so far had put us behind schedule. Sandy and Ralph said they would work with their teams on error-proofing subassembly and assembly processes. I headed inside to think.

The remaining breakfast items on the counter reminded me: lunch arrangements. Pizza two days in a row was boring, so I called Laney's Market four blocks away and ordered plates of cheeses, sliced meats, breads, and condiments. Virginia's ESP was tickling my brain, so I also asked for a veggie tray and fruit. Bags of chips and six-packs of soft drinks and water. Macadamia nut cookies for dessert. I was going whole hog today. It was either going to be a day people would remember forever for its successes, or in the other case people would at least have a good meal to compensate for a frustrating day. I was hoping for the former, but it certainly wasn't guaranteed.

Okay. Lunch taken care of. What's next? Notes about the error-proofing. Fundamentally a process issue, but the comments from Roger and Betty had gotten me thinking about the broader implications of error-proofing. A brilliant idea for categorizing error-proofing thoughts wasn't entering my head, so I opted for the obvious title on the card I wrote:

ERROR-PROOFED PROCESSES

Simplest way to achieve quality: prevent mistakes
Reduces or eliminates need for inspection (time & effort)
Reduces or eliminates rework and scrap
Results in improved efficiency & reduced resource usage
Also results in reduced cycle time

Maybe there were more benefits, but at the moment I couldn't think of any. Would increased error-proofing be enough to recover schedule today? I hoped so, but I was aware that hope was neither an answer nor a plan. At the moment I had no information justifying me pondering the issue further, so I put the card in my pocket and returned to the back yard.

I found a concerned Betty Jones waiting for me on the patio. "I'm sorry to dump this on you, Joe. My youngsters play sports every weekend. Soccer and baseball today. One of the other parents was going to drive, but he can't make it, and I'm the alternate. I need to leave, probably around lunchtime. Avery's here today, so I think he can take my place. He came up to speed real fast earlier."

"Have you talked with Avery and Zeb?"

"Yes. It's okay with them. But that's not the problem." I raised an eyebrow. *Interesting.*

"Ralph's schedule put our tree fourth for Team 3. That would finish it before lunch. Now I don't think it will be done. The delays, you know?" I did know. Schedules changing because of quality problems wasn't exactly a new experience for me. However, at the plant we normally had some time to resolve an issue. I didn't have a clue on how to finish their cat tree by lunchtime.

Of course, there was one bad option I was well aware of: behave as the plant once did when our best customer suddenly needed their order shipped immediately. Drop everything else and get everybody working on that order. Circumvent the formal system to revise assembly, subassembly, components, and internal transportation schedules for their order. Whatever was required. After the order had shipped, pick up the shattered pieces of production and attempt to restore normalcy—rescheduling all the other work that had been shoved aside because of the rush order—which always took longer than expected because of the chaos and frustration that had been created.

At the plant we don't behave that way any longer. I told Betty that I didn't know how to get her cat tree done on time, but I would try my best to find a way. Then I went in search of Ralph and Sandy to brainstorm the problem.

Both of them had finished with their teams' error-proofing process analyses. Production work was resuming, with one exception that was generating a few chuckles. Mickey was bent over, hands on knees, stymied by an interloper occupying a partially-completed cat tree. Frisky is a slinky calico cat who roams the neighborhood and thinks she owns it. She was, in true cat fashion, absorbed in cleaning her elongated back leg, ignoring Mickey's entreaties to take herself someplace else. I gently picked Frisky up from her platform and carried her to the patio table. She accepted the transfer graciously and went on with her hygiene program as though nothing had happened.

We took stools at the kitchen counter, and Ralph explained their production system. "Our system is based on smooth work flow. Balanced between processes—or functions—to eliminate delays and inventory buildup." Sounded good, but I didn't know what it had to do with getting the cat tree built.

"Different models of cat trees and scratching posts have different work content, with scratching posts taking less work than cat trees. A smooth work flow is generated by mixing production of difficult models with easy models." I said I got it. I still didn't see how this was going to produce a cat tree for Betty before lunchtime.

"To mix the models, we break down work content into small standard pieces by process—like platform subassembly, or platform carpeting. Standard blocks of work, although different models have different work content and cycle time for a block. As well as different blocks—one cat tree may have work blocks for a cat condo while another doesn't."

"Then models are sequenced so the same amount of total work from the models' blocks is in process at all times," I finished. "Roughly. I suppose you can deal with minor ups and downs." Our plant scheduling system did something similar, although probably not to the same level of detail. My impatience spilled out. "I don't see how this gets Betty's cat tree done if it was fourth in the planned sequence, but delays mean only three trees can be done before lunch."

I stood up and refilled my coffee. I remained standing, trying not to look annoyed. Deep in thought, Ralph was quiet for a short while, then said, "Has subassembly production for the second planned cat tree already started?"

"Of course," I retorted. "You're about to finish the first tree and start final assembly of the second. The subassemblies for the second need to be in process or already done."

"Right. Do you think production has already begun for the third cat tree in the planned sequence?"

I could smell a trap, so I bit back another "of course" while I considered the question.

"Probably," I said cautiously.

"Why?" Ralph asked. *Fool alert! Don't be one!* My brain synapses were firing so fast my hair likely was smoking. *Think!*

"Because of leadtime?" Ralph said. "Cycle time for the subs is so long you have to start building the third unit's subs before you have even finished the first unit's final assembly?"

"No-o-o-o-o," I said slowly. "I mean, it could be, but you broke down subassembly into small processes. Production of different subs and some processes for a specific subassembly, can run concurrently. Individual subs are less time-consuming than final assembly. Therefore, you probably don't need to build third unit subs until the second unit is in final assembly." After a bit more thought, I added, "assuming you have the items for subassembly. Which you do—carpet, wood, and so forth. They're standard items." A tiny spark of comprehension flickered into life in the back of my brain.

"Okay," Ralph said. "Because of load leveling then? Build third unit subs ahead to balance subassembly area workload?"

I was quicker this time. I shook my head. "Normally, yes, but not with your system. You balanced subassembly workload by sequencing final units." The spark was now a bright flame.

"So why would third unit subs already be in production?" Ralph persisted.

My cranium had become a conflagration. I paced the kitchen. "They aren't. We can swap the third and fourth cat trees in the schedule. Finish Betty's before lunch." I understood the system now. "Maybe we'll have to rebalance and revise the sequence for other scratching posts and cat trees. Maybe the previous third unit will become the sixth or some other position. Or maybe not—Betty's unit probably doesn't differ much in work content from the third unit. But, either way, it's planning on paper. We aren't actually jerking production around, which a reschedule normally would cause." I paused while another thought formed. "Because you defined the processes so as to build things quickly when you actually need them. You can turn on a dime."

"Well, you can't change sequence totally arbitrarily," Sandy said. "You have to operate within the general planning framework of resource and materials availability. But, yeah."

This system had possibilities for the plant. There we tended to freeze top unit schedules and roll them down to lower levels, where there were long cycle times, and workloads were balanced by building things out of sequence. What if we defined processes better and balanced workload throughout the entire production sequence? Our machinery was more complex than cat furniture, but the concept had promise. Ralph's company probably used something like it.

That was for the future, however. Right now we had to build Betty's cat tree. I chugged the last of my coffee. "Let's go. We'll tell them we can do it, then we'll do it." I led them out to the patio to deliver the good news.

*You Must Give Up The Way It Is
To Have It The Way You Want It*

GOING TO THE NEXT LEVEL

"Thanks, Joe." Betty gave a final wave, then drove away with her cat tree.

"The packaging looked different," I remarked to Zeb. "The corner protection."

"Yeah," he said. "We made the cardboard pieces easier for people to flatten out when they get home. If we're lucky, the cardboard will end up in recycle bins instead of garbage cans."

"Good idea." We joined everybody else preparing and consuming sandwiches. I made a salami-and-swiss on dark rye.

Ralph had quickly gobbled his lunch and was hard at work on his computer. "Still replanning?" I asked between bites.

"Updating process definitions," he said. "Eliminating inspections for processes that are now error-proofed. Also using templates to generate processes for Avery's and Kim's new models of cat trees."

I completely forgot about their requests for modified cat trees! "What do you mean?"

"Processes for building platforms and attaching platforms to cat trees are standard," he said, taking a break from his keyboard. "I just need to generate one-off designs for different size platforms and different numbers of platforms on a tree. Process-based design. Where possible, using standard processes to build things. Dimensions, materials, labor content, and other elements can vary, but process steps are standard. Great for designing, planning, training—numerous advantages for improving quality." He refocused on his screen.

Another good idea. Which reminded me that I hadn't documented the previous good idea either. The first DESIGN FOR PRODUCTION index card was full, so I made a second:

DESIGN FOR PRODUCTION #2

Where possible, make standard processes parameter-based.
- same process steps used for different materials, sizes, and so forth

Designs should facilitate balanced flow and low cycle time
- improves customer responsiveness: schedule changes, customer order changes, etc.

I wasn't sure I had captured the substance of everything I had learned in the previous two hours, but my attention was interrupted by the sound of Virginia's car pulling into the driveway. I and most of the production team members hurried around the house to find out what had transpired with Buzzy. Ralph and a few others continued with their activities.

My wife was worn out, but the tension lines had left her face. "He had a bad muscle spasm in his back that affected the rear legs. Took some time to get in to see the right vet, then I had to wait to make sure the painkillers and muscle relaxants took effect. He's a lot better, but still pretty much out of it." I looked into the cat carrier. Buzzy was curled up asleep, looking like a beach ball of long caramel and black hair.

I carried him into my office and gently set him down by the food and water that were still there. He purred, which melted our hearts. We moved a litter box nearby. Virginia showed me two vials of pills. "One of each twice a day. Oh, joy!" Most cats don't like taking pills, and Buzzy is no exception. That's when you find out their reactions are like lightning and their little pointed fangs are really, really sharp.

"Do I want to know how much this journey to Platinum Vet Land cost?" I asked. "No," Virginia said sweetly as she left the room. "Just don't plan on retiring any time soon."

The office window showed me that activities had resumed in the back yard after people learned that Buzzy was going to be okay. I saw Ralph and Luis carrying my table saw from the garage to a position where it could supply cat tree production. I hadn't realized the implications of the requests for different size platforms, that there would be a need to cut some wood pieces to augment the standard-sized pieces that were precut and delivered last week. What would we do without Ralph? He thinks of everything.

I sat beside Buzzy and petted him for a while, glad he was mending and enjoying a brief respite from the back yard battles. The peace lasted for ten minutes until Ralph appeared at the office doorway and said he and Luis needed to see me.

Luis had been test-cutting with a few pieces of scrap plywood. "There's something wrong with the saw, Mr. Hall. It stops before the cut is completely made. The blade just stops spinning and winds down."

I pointed to two small plastic pieces attached to the sides of the table, projecting two inches into the air. "You see those? Refugee components from a home security system. They shoot a light beam across the table two inches in front of the blade. The beam is an inch above the table, high enough to let a board under but too low for your hand. An optical interlock so you can't cut a finger off. You have to use a pusher board behind the board you're cutting." I demonstrated.

"I'm careful, Mr. Hall, and I've had training," Luis objected. "I don't need those things."

"Everybody is careful," I said. "Do you think anybody intentionally cuts off a finger or falls off a ladder? Safety isn't only about being careful and being trained. It's about removing the possibility of mistakes and the injuries they cause."

"Trust him," Ralph said. "He's right." We left Luis to continue his testing. Ralph congratulated me on the interlock. "Nice system, Joe. I'll install one on my table saw."

"Thanks." I asked him about his revised design and process documentation. "I need to get it into my computer and print it out for the teams to use instead of whatever they're using in the interim for immediate implementation of the changes. Red-lined drawings and instructions, I presume?"

"Right. I already emailed the documentation to you." To my inquiring glance, he said, "Wireless. Sandy will send hers when she's done with the work for Team 2." He pointed to her typing intensely at a computer on the patio table.

I thanked him and went to my office to retrieve the email. Ralph's work was complete and clear (of course) and I had no difficulty incorporating it into the 'official' documentation. While I was working, Sandy's email arrived, so I included her modifications, too. It took me a little over an hour to finish it all, including the printing and proofreading. I didn't want to take a chance on affecting Buzzy's recuperation, so I just let the classical station play softly in the background while I updated the documentation. I took a couple of mental health breaks for coffee, clearing my head by changing gears—checking out things in the back yard. The ash and silver maple trees needed pruning to keep them channeling their nutrition productively into healthy buds and leaves. More germane to the project, I saw Avery had replaced Betty effectively on Team 3. Neither Avery's presence nor Betty's absence had been foreseen. Sometimes things just work out if you let them.

When Virginia returned, I drank my first mocha; she had thoughtfully brought me two—non fat, of course. We watched Frisky stalk a squirrel on the back fence. When she got too close, the squirrel would scamper away, and the cat would patiently resume her creeping towards it. As a younger cat, Buzzy pursued squirrels for a while, too. Until one day when the frustrated squirrel turned around and beat the stuffing out of him. Squirrels are tough little buggers. For them, being alert and hardy isn't a game as it is for the cat; it's a matter of survival. There's probably a lesson of some kind in that story. Perhaps Frisky was going to learn it today. Most of us learn that way—from experience. I hoped she wouldn't get hurt. Or not hurt more seriously than experience hurts most of us.

Carrying my second mocha (I had to admit, the non fat version didn't taste that bad), I took the revised documentation to the production teams. Sandy, Ralph, Mary and Zeb were having a serious discussion about something. Close to them, another group was listening to Roger expostulate, arms waving in his usual exuberant fashion. Some people, but not many, were still working.

"Glueing," Mary said when I inquired. "We've made enough cat trees now to know that we need better instructions for glueing carpet to platforms. It's too easy to use too much or too little glue, or to apply it in too many places or too few."

Avery broke off listening to Roger and came over to our group. "We need to do some serious error-proofing of the glueing process. Tell people the right way to do it." He explained his suggestion for measuring out the precise amount of glue needed to attach a carpet piece and applying drops precisely in the center of each small square in a grid that would be drawn on the wood—or possibly on the back of the carpet. Clearly the idea would work. It also clearly would at least double the time to perform the glueing.

By now the other group had drifted over. All of them except one—Roger—agreed with Avery. They were seriously charged up with the concept of error-proofing.

"You have an opinion, Joe?" Mary asked.

Before I could respond, Roger burst out, "That's crazy! It's overkill! We don't need that kind of precision!"

"We want to do it right," Avery argued.

"Perhaps there are alternative ways to do it right," Ralph said diplomatically. "In some circumstances there can be process variance—noticeable, measurable variance—yet production can be defect-free. There can be an amount of acceptable process variance."

"That's what I'm saying!" Roger cried. "In my job I have to make coffee drinks with the milk at 170 degrees. But it doesn't matter if the temperature is 169 or 172. That's okay."

"How do you know it isn't 180?" Avery asked. "You want to scald someone?"

"The thermometer has a green colored range of acceptable temperatures. As long as the needle is in the range, I'm okay."

"Like a fire extinguisher," somebody said. "The gauge tells you when it's okay and when it needs recharging." Roger nodded. "Yes. Something like that."

"What do you suggest?" I asked Roger.

"I don't know. I'm not an engineer. Some sort of simple pattern for where to lay down a strip of glue."

Luis was done with his test-cutting (and, by now, probably with his real cutting). He had been listening to the discussion. "I've got an idea," he said. He pulled a black felt-tip pen from his pocket. "How about this?" He drew a pattern on a piece of cardboard:

"I don't know how many turns there should be," he said, "or the width of the bands, but you get the idea. We know the glue applicator lays down a uniform bead. So we just need to control the placement of the bead. As long as the person gets the bead within the lines of the pattern, they've done okay."

"Like control charts," Avery mused.

"What are those?" Roger and Luis said in stereo.

"The full name is Statistical Process Control charts. SPC. Basically a process operator—or a computer—measures and keeps track of a key process variable. Like temperature. Milk temperature in Roger's job. Welding head temperature in our plant. And pressure. Lots of things."

"If the variable is within a certain range, it's okay," said Roger. "Like my milk temperature within the green range.

"Right," Avery confirmed. "If the value falls outside the range, the operator shuts down the process and fixes it. Or the process shuts down automatically."

"How is the range of acceptable values established?"

"Statistics and history. As Ralph said, the notion is to know the process range within which 100% good product will be produced. It isn't a statistically acceptable level of defects. It is a statistical and experiential method to produce items with zero defects. It would probably work with the glueing."

"As long as the glue line falls within the glue control bands," Mary said, "the carpet piece is satisfactorily glued. If it strays outside the band, we stop and redo the work."

I have never really understood control charts, and I knew I had probably just heard the explanation for idiots. However, I knew a lot more than I had before. "Thanks, Avery."

He gave a curt nod. "You're welcome, Joe."

"As a practical matter," Zeb asked, "how are we going to establish the width and pattern of our glue control bands?"

Ralph said he would be inclined to rely on experience of the teams so far. "You know what has worked, and what hasn't worked. You primarily need a process that ensures the glueing person only applies glue in a way that will work."

"You could define control bands scientifically," said Avery. "I'm sure the adhesive manufacturer has detailed specifications on bonding strength per quantity applied to standard surface areas of various materials."

Everybody except Ralph and Sandy looked as though Avery had just uttered a sentence in ancient Greek. "Not this time, Avery," I said. "Maybe on the next project."

"So," Zeb said. "What do we do now?"

Sandy suggested, "Redraw Luis's pattern to match your experience. Make templates. Start using them to apply the adhesive to the carpet. Expand the idea to the posts."

"Okay," Zeb responded. "Let's get moving." He took charge, and Luis was soon the center of a discussion group. I headed for the house to incorporate the concept into the instructions. I saw Mary carry her computer to the patio table and open it up. I assumed that Sandy had asked her to record the template decision. "You don't need to do that," I said. "I'll take care of the documentation."

"I'm doing something else," she said. She opened her mouth to speak, then closed it. Sandy came up beside her. "Go ahead, you can show it to him. We've got the bugs out." Mary gave her an uncertain look, then called up a spreadsheet on the screen. She sipped her water, then described the display.

"The rows list the requirements—all of them—customer, regulations, whatever. The columns list how a requirement will be met, from design spec through obsolescence and disposal. In this case, the requirement for firm carpet attachment."

"The columns also include how a requirement is verified as being met," Sandy added. "Design validations, production inspections, error-proofed processes, whatever. It makes sure nothing falls through the cracks. Compliance with the requirements is verified through every step. Just a notation that a requirement has been met, of course. Actual compliance evidence is in subsidiary documents like inspection records."

"A lot of work," I said. *But it would have prevented last month's problem with the Sanderson order where we just plain overlooked their requirement for the special coating.*

"Worth it," Sandy said. "If you want defect-free products."

"Probably so." I saw the stern look on her face and corrected myself. "Definitely so." I went to my office, brain whirling like a hamster wheel.

When I came into the room, I saw that Buzzy had awakened from his nap. He looked at me groggily, then slowly pushed himself to his feet and wobbled towards me. I sat on the floor and fed him some cat treats from the palm of my hand. After eating a few, he lay down, started his purring motor, and closed his eyes. Soon he was fast asleep again.

I updated process documentation to the accompaniment of an elevator music station, which I figured wouldn't disturb Buzzy's dreams. After finishing the documentation update, I added a line to the ERROR-PROOFED PROCESSES note card:

Some processes need to be satisfactory, not perfect
  – keep process variance within acceptable range
  – use experience or statistics to establish range

I thought about the compliance table that Mary and Sandy had created. It didn't take much verbiage to record the concept:

REQUIREMENTS COMPLIANCE

Document plans to achieve compliance
Document attainment of compliance
- actual compliance evidence in separate records

Done with the cards, I gazed out at the scene in the back yard. People were productive and happy. The day was finally coming together.

**See The Simple In The Complex:
See The Great In The Small**

PROJECT DONE—HOPEFULLY

I toured the back yard, which looked like the Oregon Trail after thousands of settlers had passed in their prairie schooners. I noticed many processes were still not error-proofed and required inspection. "That's normal," Ralph assured me. "It takes a long time to make production processes bulletproof. In the meantime you eliminate defects through inspection and rework." Sandy added, "You never get to perfect processes—you always find ways to make them even better." After a couple more turns around the yard, I realized I was getting in people's way, not contributing anything. Ralph and Sandy confirmed my opinion that the production was zipping along smoothly. I made a pot of coffee, which Sandy and I shared at the patio table while Ralph drank club soda.

"It's going very well," I remarked. "Not much for us bosses to do."

"I think we could find something," Ralph said cryptically.

"You think stirring the pot is a good idea? We could just let people enjoy themselves."

"On the other hand," Ralph replied, "they could continue improving and go home sooner. Or build another cat tree for themselves. Complacency is seldom a useful attitude."

I looked at Sandy in mock amazement. "Is he this way Monday through Friday, too?"

"We all are," she said. "And I'll bet you are, too, if there really is a new Joe."

"You've got a point," I admitted. "So what do you guys have in mind?" They reminded me that my focus was quality, not production, and humorously said that surely there was something I could do on quality instead of worrying about their production system. I pretended outrage, but actually they were right. My subconscious was bugging me about the whole notion of production process assurance. So I took the coffee inside and walked down to my office.

Buzzy was still sleeping on the floor. Virginia had left for one of her volunteer activities at a local charity. I mused about what I had learned on production processes—the implications of doing them right the first time versus eliminating errors through detection and rework. Realizing there was a basic principle involved, I wrote a card without a title:

Joe's First Law:	100% defect-free output requires either a controlled process or 100% inspection.
Joe's Second Law:	controlled processes in the long run are a better solution than inspection (less expensive, lower cycle time)

Through the window I saw Sandy and Ralph push their chairs back from the patio table and stand up. Sandy nodded at something Ralph said, then they walked together to the right side of the yard and disappeared from my view. I wondered what they were doing and almost went out to ask until I remembered that I was supposed to be working on quality. I was trying to invent something to do when the phone rang. This time the cordless handset was on my desk. I thought it might be Junior calling, so I snatched it up quickly.

"Could I speak to the primary person who makes the telecommunication decisions in the household?" Sales call.

"I would be happy to get him for you," I said, "but he has a bad muscle spasm in his back and is sleeping. He is on heavy medication. Could I have him call you in a few days when he's feeling better?"

"No problem, sir. I'll call back." They hung up. Virginia thinks it is rude when I behave this way to people who are only trying to make a living any way they can. I know she's right, but sometimes I can't help it. Some deep character flaw.

Feeling guilty but happy (or happy but guilty), I returned my attention to the back yard. My eyes wandered over the production teams until they landed on Zeb's area. I recalled the first time I had seen him this morning. *Aha! Something for me to do!* I went out to check on Zeb's revised cleanup program. The plant was neater than it had ever been, but we certainly didn't have all the answers, and I had no doubt that a messy workplace hindered high quality. Maybe Zeb had learned something today we could use.

I was aware that I had seen no piles of debris today and I was amazed at how tidy the work areas actually were. And how compact the team work areas were. Production and transportation work on subassemblies and final assembly was taking place with a truly impressive economy of motion.

"The team leaders worked together on a solution," Zeb said. "People are now responsible for cleaning their own work spaces. We agreed on rules for keeping anything—tools, material, cleaning rags, whatever—in a production area. And how to store it. We want to bring something into a production area when we need it, put it in a handy place, then remove it when it's no longer needed—instead of stepping around it constantly." I said the approach obviously was working, and he flashed a big smile from the depths of his bushy beard.

Mary came over, and she and Zeb agreed that it was a good time for a break. While people washed up, I helped with getting soft drinks from the house and garage refrigerators to the patio, and I brought out the lunch leftovers. There were even a few breakfast items left from the carload Virginia had bought when the sun was in the east instead of the west.

I talked with almost everybody about how things were going in their opinion. Happiness and unhappiness are both contagious, and I prefer the former. I didn't expect universal bubbling glee. After all, people have their own personalities, and you have to respect that. My best barometer of the degree of negative attitude was Roger, but he didn't have much criticism left in him. Being right about the glueing process management had melted most of his prickliness. Sometimes all any of us needs is a little bit of praise.

I mentally reviewed what I had seen in the production areas and what Zeb had told me. It was more than we did at the plant. Out of my pocket came a pen and a card that soon read:

EFFECTIVE (QUALITY) WORKPLACE

Clean work area; no trash, debris, dirt
Arrange tools & materials for easy access
Remove items not needed for current work
Discipline to maintain work area
Standard procedures performed routinely

Ralph and Sandy came into the kitchen wearing determined expressions. "We wanted to talk with you before the break ended." They told me what they had been thinking and doing. It seemed to me that they had a good idea, so we decided to give it a go. I was elected ringleader.

On the patio I waved my arm in a circle over my head to get everybody's attention. (Being tall can definitely be an asset.) "We have some options for proceeding from here on. We can carry on as we have been, or we can try to figure out how to be even more productive and perhaps go home sooner. Or even build more cat trees and scratching posts if you'd like."

I knew there were introverted people in the group who would be silent unless their pants were on fire, but there were also go-getters like Ann. "Why don't we see how much we can do?" she asked. Melissa agreed, "Awesome." Other comments came from people who felt similarly, including several who liked what they were doing today and wanted more furniture for their four-footed friends.

"How can we do that?" I asked. Sandy and Ralph had shared some possibilities with me, but we all felt that ideas would have more staying power if they came from the group.

"More process error-proofing," somebody said. "Less time spent on inspections and rework."

"Can't," somebody else replied. "We did all that we could. For now, anyway." After a short discussion, agreement was reached that further error-proofing today was unlikely.

"Then how about faster response to failed inspections?" Kim suggested. "Sometimes error correction requires a person with a special skill to stop their work and help with the rework." Agreement was reached to develop a rapid response capability. Ralph said he could provide a potential technique.

"If we're going to build more posts and trees, we need to know how productive we're being," Mickey said reasonably. "How fast we're making them, and how many. So we know if we can get them all finished—that rework isn't killing us."

"Basically we need to know if we're producing to the schedule that the balanced work is based on," Avery said.

It was good to see that he had bought into the total system. His rapid education validated the training tools. He continued. "If we're on the schedule, then it also means that the work balancing is effective and we're being efficient."

"If we're not on schedule, we need to know why," Kim said. "Where we are behind. And the reasons."

Sandy stepped up beside me and asked if people were finding the INSPECTION STATUS boards to be useful. There was a consensus that the boards were very informative. Sandy suggested expanding the content to include production output performance for each subassembly and assembly work area, including estimates of projected future output. "We'll know if we're behind schedule. Or there is unused capacity."

"And where there are flow problems," Luis added. "Or I suppose just generally if there are flow imbalances."

"Correct," Ralph said. "Flow improvements never end."

Everybody was pumped up over the opportunity for even higher output, or to go home early, or both. There was a moment of group trepidation when a question about materials was asked, but I assured everybody that the schedule would provide enough time to procure materials not in stock.

People who wanted additional pieces of cat furniture worked with Ralph on updating the production sequence to include new items as well as previously-planned items. Sandy took Ann and a member of each of the other teams, and they set about expanding the INSPECTION STATUS boards to PRODUCTION STATUS boards. I grabbed my car keys and went to buy the few additional materials we would need.

I returned to find that Melissa had been to her car to retrieve a boom box and CDs. The music playing loudly was by an artist recognizable only by someone under the age of 18 or their patient parents. Everybody seemed happy, so I decided the new Joe would not waste mental energy on the music.

Ralph had distributed the revised production sequence, and schedule information had been transferred to the white boards. I asked Ralph if I could do anything to help with the rapid response to problems that he had mentioned.

"The primary objective," he said, "is to create instant awareness of a problem and obtain immediate assistance for its resolution. Other objectives, if we choose, can be additional knowledge and data collection regarding problems. What do you have around the house that we could use for alerting people when a problem arises?"

"You mean like a whistle?" I asked.

"Sounds are good, as long as they are not disruptive or too non-directional. The response must be focused as well as fast."

"So something visual might be better in our situation."

"Could be," he said, and I considered the alternatives.

An idea occurred to me. "I have some tiki torches in the garage for summer evening parties. Basically six-foot poles with pointed ends to stick in the ground. And red flags for when I carry lumber that sticks out beyond the tailgate of my truck. How about a red flag on a pole to indicate a problem?"

"Perfect." He and I went to get the materials. Ten minutes later people had been briefed on the use of red flags, to supplement their briefings on maintaining the PRODUCTION STATUS white boards. The teams now had effective production processes, production plans, and an information system for communication and action. The boom box belted out hip-hop music while increased production began in earnest.

I was busy for a while, assisting Ralph, Sandy, and the team leaders with resolving problems, mostly minor, and implementation of the expanded white boards and red flags. Faster than I had expected, however, people got the hang of using the white boards as effective communication devices. The red flags too proved to be valuable; people responded to the raising of a red flag like an ambulance team to a 10-car pileup. It wasn't long before production was flowing so smoothly that I moved to the patio to watch and drink coffee.

That soon became boring, so I went into my office and documented the red flags and white boards, alternating that work with petting Buzzy and feeding him treats. Through the window I watched Sandy and Ralph traveling from team to team, offering assistance as necessary.

I was thankful for Sandy's and Ralph's assistance with the visual alert and status system. I made up a new card:

COMMUNICATION

People are most effective when they know what's going on
Interactive visual tools are useful to:
- inform and provide direction
- initiate improvement action (quality, performance, safety, etc.)
- resolve problems (quality, performance, safety, etc.)

I had answered the sales call because it might have been Junior. I decided not to wait further for the phone to ring—I am not by nature a passive person. I called him to see if he would tell me why he and Rachel were coming over tonight. He declined. "Sorry, Dad. Some things are best discussed face-to-face. See you in a few hours." His response, of course, drove me up the wall. I went to the kitchen, got more coffee and watched production standing at the kitchen counter. Sandy came in for her coffee refill, and I remarked that it was amazing how well Ralph had done on his estimates of times for subassembly and assembly production. "I don't see anybody out there standing around waiting for work, or looking rushed to finish their work."

"It's partially time estimates, Joe," she said, helping herself to one of the remaining lunch cookies. "But the main reason is triggering of production from higher-up demand. Final assembly operations of one unit trigger top subassembly start for the next unit. And so on down to materials pulling. If production runs a bit slower or faster than the theoretical times, the system absorbs the variation because subsequent production is triggered slower or faster. Unforeseen things can happen to speed up or slow down production." She raised an eyebrow to see if I got it.

Like Avery substituting for Betty. "But you still have to meet the overall schedule," I said, trying not to leave a question mark at the end of my statement.

"Of course. We measure output continually and take whatever action is necessary to get the planned work done in the planned total time period. Like getting today's cat furniture completed today."

"Speaking of which, I assume it's going well overall?" She had some cookie crumbs on her upper lip, so I pantomimed rubbing stuff off my lip.

She cleaned her lip with a paper towel. "Thanks. Yeah, we're a bit ahead overall. Our best guess is probably around 4:30 for everything to be done."

"'Informed estimate,' you mean," I said smiling. "Yes," she smiled back and returned to the back yard factory.

Through my office window I kept up with production while I made my way through an operations management book; you have to know when not to help people as well as when to help. I know this even though I don't do it all the time. At 4:26 the final cat tree was done, and the teams moved fully into packaging and protection mode for transport of the furniture to its new residence and new furry owners. I went out to assist where I could, even if only with loading furniture into vehicles.

"I can't thank you enough, Joe," Avery said as he closed the back hatch on his SUV. "It's been a great day."

"A great weekend," Mary said as her daughter got into the passenger side of her car. "Sure beat building shelves." Ellis went by, nodding his head and agreeing. I felt good for myself and proud of the work the teams had done.

Kim, Mickey, Luis, and everybody else also expressed their delight with the furniture and the experience of constructing it. Roger's eyes were moist with gratitude for the cat tree he couldn't have afforded to buy.

Ralph and Sandy helped me clean up the back yard and put tools back in the garage, then they joined Virginia and me for an early dinner. We went to a casual family restaurant where people won't be embarrassed showing up in the clothes in which they have worked all day. I decided that taking care of my health wasn't such a bad idea, so I had fish. Conversation around the table was good, although Ralph was a bit subdued. I wondered if the smashing success of the project had been a bit unexpected for him, perhaps indicating that my company might become more of a quality threat to his company than he had thought. *Probably total fantasy to think that way. Yeah, but it feels good, so tonight I'll let myself do it.*

Junior and Rachel arrived at the house about ten minutes after Ralph and Sandy had left—just enough time to make coffee and put the last of the lunch cookies on a plate. I was nervous. Virginia was dealing with the prospective discussion much better than I was. "Whatever it is, darling, we'll help them, and all of us will get through it together as a family."

It was apparent that our son and his wife were nervous, too. They sat very close together on the sofa while the four of us made small talk, drank coffee, and ate cookies. Actually, the three of them only nibbled cookies. I inhaled three of them and about a quart of coffee. *At least they're probably not separating. They wouldn't be cuddled up together if they were having problems.*

I realized what was left for a major family discussion. Either their financial ruin or serious illness. *More coffee. I need more coffee.* I went to the kitchen to put on another pot.

When I returned, everyone was sitting quietly. *Okay, must be time to get to the main topic.* I sat down and was quiet.

Junior and Rachel sat forward on the sofa. They clasped hands. "Mom and Dad," Junior said hesitantly, "we have good news and bad news." *Here it comes.* "I got a job as Production Manager for a different company. It's a small company, but the position is a nice step up for me. And it pays pretty well." *Okay, so what's the problem?* "Unfortunately, it's not in this town. Not in this state, actually. But we'll only be a few hours away." He looked at me apprehensively.

Virginia threw me a quick glance while a small smile played on her face. It was touching that Junior and Rachel enjoyed living close to us—as we enjoyed it, too—but we had known it was only a matter of time until one of them received a better job offer someplace else. I was pleased for them, but I knew I shouldn't act too pleased. I delayed responding longer than I should have, which of course worried them.

"Dad," Rachel said, "We know this is a big shock, but we'll visit often. We promise. Honestly."

"Of course you will," Virginia said firmly. "We're delighted to hear the news. It was just a surprise." *Nice cover for my fumbling.* I got my act together and congratulated my son. The four of us talked for a while longer. They were both upbeat about the move. Rachel already had a couple of job possibilities lined up in the new city. She is very marketable, and I am sure the day is coming when she and Junior will be relocating because of an opportunity for her.

Junior was understandably nervous about his new responsibilities. "I think I can do the job," he said, "but the scope is a bit overwhelming. All of Production. The company is small with not a lot of people—at least compared to your plant. But there are still a lot of functions and departments."

I hesitated before I answered, uncertain as to how my reply would be taken. Finally I plunged ahead. "Son, the last thing in the world I want is to be pushy. This is your life. But if I can ever be helpful, just ask. Please."

His eyes met mine directly. "I'd like that, Dad. Seriously. I have a lot to learn. Thanks. Can I ask you a couple of things now?" I said Sure. Virginia and Rachel went into the kitchen, and my son and I spent twenty minutes or so discussing what he was probably going to have to look into during the first few days after he found his office in the new place. We agreed to talk further as often as he wanted.

After they went home, Virginia cleaned up the few dishes. As she loaded the dishwasher, she said, "Guess what? They're thinking of starting a family."

I was amazed. "You're kidding. Rachel's quitting work? With the fast track she's on?"

Virginia shook her head. "Different world from ours, dear. They're both going to continue working while raising the child."

I pondered that briefly, considering how the new Joe should react. "Okay. I guess. If there is one thing I've learned in the past year—or should have learned—it's that I don't know everything, and there is always room for new ideas. I suppose that's actually two things, but both are true."

"You're right," she said. "They'll be fine. Now it's bedtime. You've had a long and tough day."

"Soon," I said. "One thing left to do." I went to my office to update my journal for the day's events. In addition to transcribing the new cards, I added a line to the BASIC PRINCIPLES paragraph to memorialize the importance of the fantastic teamwork that had been displayed today:

> Everybody needs to be on board—top management to individual contributors

After I had finished the journal entries, I skimmed the entire list of my thoughts on quality. It looked pretty thorough. I was sure the journal would be useful at the plant. I closed it, did a final check on Buzzy, and went to bed.

I was exhausted and fell asleep immediately. I dreamed of big cats again, but this time they were docile and playful with me, including their cubs. Didn't take a Freud or Jung to interpret that dream: I was happy with how everything had turned out that day, with the project and with family, and I foresaw nothing but smooth sailing ahead.

For once I was more or less correct.

When The Student Is Ready,
The Teacher Will Appear

Your Self-Worth Must Be Stronger Than The Rejection Of Your Ideas By Others

REALITY CHECK

For a couple of weeks I received accolades by email, at the supermarket, and everywhere I ran across people who had worked on the project or knew somebody who had. I would be lying if I said I wasn't pleased, but I knew that mainly I had been in the right place at the right time. More important was the practical knowledge I had gained on designing and building a quality product. You would wonder what I had been smoking if I told you producing complex machinery at the plant was the same as building cat furniture in my back yard, but there were a number of lessons I learned for which the quality concepts, and some of the specific techniques, proved to be transferable.

Some families needed clarification on matters such as acceptable cleaning products for the cat furniture (basically any non-toxic household cleaner). Other people wanted to know more about materials and construction of the scratching posts and cat trees—probably to assure themselves that the products actually were as good as commercially available products. They were in fact far superior, so providing the data was a pleasure.

I had received information from all the relevant federal and state agencies (very cooperative), and had investigated other external sources for suggestions on product requirements. We ended up with few revisions, and of course the revisions and compliance with requirements both were recorded in our files.

I returned emails and telephone calls almost every day until Kim and another teenage computer genius set up a web site with information about the furniture and the capability to send and receive email. We spread customer contact responsibility among several of us from the project. I and others made house calls to customers who needed the personal touch.

I recorded the customer support lesson in my journal:

CUSTOMER SUPPORT

Complete documentation for customer
  – use, maintenance, disposal instructions
  – information to answer any reasonable question
Rapid response to customer:
  – questions, inquiries for information
  – requests for assistance

Over the next several months the seeds sown by me and the production teams sprouted and grew in the community. The prospect of obtaining quality cat scratching posts and climbing trees for much less than store prices appealed to many people. Some invested their own time in production. Others paid to have the work done by people who had worked on the project. Ann recruited friends to learn cat furniture construction, and they turned out items for school and church fund-raisers. The volume of web site hits grew dramatically.

Naturally we made improvements in product designs and production processes. A number of revisions sprung from our own gray matter, and others resulted from customer experience and feedback. Internally-generated improvements included a tougher but less expensive brand of carpet (actually produced by a well-known carpet manufacturer but available in this brand only over the Internet) and placement of brackets that better reflected the actual 'stress vectors' (words I do not really understand—courtesy of Kim's father who turned out to be a mechanical engineer) impinging on the platforms.

We discovered that tipping over the cat trees was not an impossibility; customers reported that a couple of determined or rambunctious felines could do the job. But they didn't seem to tip over in a predictable way. We performed a Root Cause Analysis and determined that the particular configuration of a cat tree—size of platforms or cat condos, their number, their height on the central post, and so forth—would make it more likely to tip in one direction than another. Then we broadened the base in the appropriate direction to improve stability, making the cat tree equally stable in all directions. Which basically eliminated any potential concerns, since there had never been a general problem of instability.

As time passed, customers contributed suggestions for product features. Production and design experience of our cat furniture teams led to ideas for product revisions. We also saw commercial cat furniture makers doing different things. We prioritized everything using the 80/20 Rule or A–B–C Classification or Pareto's Law (the vital few versus the trivial many)—whatever term you like. We documented requirements, analyzed them, evaluated alternative design approaches, and so on through to prototyping of production processes. Eventually production and support of the updated products in a manner that unequivocally achieved compliance with product requirements.

The simple fact of living with a product—as a customer, designer, or builder—sparks the mind's creative powers to figure out ways to make the product better. I added a concept to my journal, in the **BASIC PRINCIPLES** section, to reflect the importance of experience and the passage of time:

The product's design & production processes can always be improved
- from customer feedback
- from internal ideas
- from competitors' products
- from other external sources, e.g. laws

I included the final line because it was clear to me that society's interest in product safety and so forth could only increase. In fact, there was a general principle at work here: quality is a journey with no destination and no time frame for completion. The road stretches to the horizon and beyond. None of us will in our lifetime be able to do more than be responsible travelers who also took time to enjoy the scenery.

I was happy at work. The plant's quality is getting better all the time. I doubt Ralph and his colleagues are yet sending out resumés, but they know we are closing the quality gap.

Junior and Rachel love their jobs. We see them as often as possible, but not often enough. Such is the way of the world.

Virginia is happy and busy, too (same thing to her). Buzzy lives the contented life of a feline elder statesman. None of us has any clue as to what life holds. We can't see around the next bend, but we know that we will be able to deal with—and enjoy—whatever the universe sets in our path.

Local Man Is Santa Claws

by J. B. Hickok, *Staff Writer*

METRO — Christmas came early for neighbors and friends of resident Joe Hall. They received gifts for their pet cats almost for free. The price was their labor and a small charge for materials.

Mr. Hall, an executive with a local manufacturing firm, organized a project to build "cat furniture" for pets owned by neighbors. "Our cat climbing tree has more features than the ones we purchased," commented Dr. Deborah Crockett, a physician and avid fan of the project, in which her son participated. "It's a better quality scratching post than anything you can get in a store or from a catalog," raved Roger Holliday, another neighbor. "Joe taught us how to do it ourselves. He really understands quality."

Since the initial weekend effort a few months ago, teen-agers who built furniture for their cuddly companions have bragged to their school friends. Adults talked up the project to coworkers, at poker parties, on the golf course, and at virtually every social event. As a result, Mr. Hall conducted several additional weekend production sessions for cat lovers, but the demand for the cat furniture seems nowhere near satisfied.

Awareness of the home-made products has reached the largest local pet store, where employees are very impressed. "It's the highest quality cat furniture any of us has ever seen," said store manager Clay Masterson. "At a great price. And customers have a huge variety of options. These local people could put the national companies out of business."

When asked to comment, Joe Hall said, "I'm flattered. I have had the opportunity to work with tremendous people in our neighborhood and the entire city. I don't know where this effort will ultimately lead, but I'm looking forward to enjoying every day of the adventure."

***Whatever You Give Your Energy To
Is What You Will Have More Of***

JOE'S JOURNAL

Following are the journal entries transcribed from my index card notes. They are reorganized slightly from the order in which the cards were originally written, and a few ideas have been expanded upon slightly.

BASIC PRINCIPLES

Efficient responsive production and high quality
    production are two views of the same gem
Quality is meeting requirements for the particular product
Take subjectivity out of quality
Everybody needs to be on board—top management to
    individual contributors
Product design & production processes can always be improved
    — from customer feedback
    — from internal ideas
    — from competitors products
    — from other external sources, e.g. laws

PRODUCT REQUIREMENTS
Include customer, end user, and relevant third parties
- third parties may be government, consumer groups, standards organizations, professional societies, etc.
- may include consideration of third parties who come in contact with product, e.g. transport firms

Include internal standards beyond external requirements
- where external requirements may be lacking or we have higher standards, such as higher performance, higher reliability , or lower cost

Cover entire life cycle of product
Document as clearly and quantitatively as possible
- includes criteria for knowing requirements are met

DESIGN FOR REQUIREMENTS
Translate product requirements into design specifications
- specs must be unambiguous
- must be clear link from requirement to spec

Create designs to meet specifications
- must know how to measure spec compliance
- must document that designs satisfy specifications

Requirements & specifications rolled down from level to level in structure of product, i.e. final unit to lower level subassemblies to raw materials
Develop design rules for orderly design process

DESIGN FOR PRODUCTION
Design should match production capabilities & processes
- includes standards for process safety, environmental impact, etc.

Make design easy to produce right, difficult to do wrong
Minimal No. of Parts–Standard Parts.
- standard means proven, known to work.

Standard processes where possible: best practices
Production prototyping–all critical products & processes
Where possible, make standard processes parameter- based.
- same process steps used for different materials, product sizes, and so forth

Designs should facilitate balanced flow and low cycle time
- improves customer responsiveness: schedule changes, customer options, etc.

Basically covers making the product and delivering it to the customer (plus maintenance we're responsible for)
Design documentation complete and detailed
- includes validation that objectives are met

PRODUCTION INSTRUCTIONS
All designs and processes documented
- graphically and in simple writing

Include everything needed to build it well
- all necessary steps
- resource capabilities, e.g. people, tools, equipment
- all required materials, parts, supplies

Instructions need to be complete and clear
Use standard instructions—referenced, not repeated
Checklist to make sure nothing is left out

PRODUCTION PROCESSES

Production processes consistent with inspection methods
   - products built with processes will pass inspection
Approved processes documented and explained clearly
Production prototyping—all critical products & processes

ERROR-PROOFED PROCESSES

Simplest way to achieve quality: prevent mistakes
Production processes should reduce chance of errors
   - ideally processes designed to eliminate errors
Reduces or eliminates need for inspection (time & effort)
Reduces or eliminates rework and scrap
Results in improved efficiency & reduced resource usage
Also results in reduced cycle time
Some processes need to be satisfactory, not perfect
   - keep process variance within acceptable range
   - use experience or statistics to establish range

INSPECTION/TEST

Necessary when processes are not error-proofed
   - do not pass on defective work to next process
Measure to objective standards known to all
Use agreed-upon measuring tools/processes
Inspection standards consistent with specifications
   - include all specifications that must be met
Simple, standard inspection procedures & tools
   - error-proofed tools such as templates
   - tools certified & maintained accurately
Point-of-production inspection
   - minimize rework and delays
   - correct process before more work is started

PROCESS ASSURANCE
Joe's First Law: 100% defect-free output requires either a controlled process or 100% inspection.
Joe's Second Law: controlled processes in the long run are a better solution than inspection (less expensive, lower cycle time)

QUALITY-RESOURCES
Align resource capabilities with tasks to be done
- verified/certified capabilities
- avoid over-qualified as well as under-qualified

Make sure equipment and tools don't cause problems
- conduct preventive maintenance (PM) program
- periodically inspect and re-certify non-PM items
- make sure people understand routine care

Consider short-term and long-term needs
- surge capacity as well as sustained capacity

Don't forget support functions that impact production

EFFECTIVE (QUALITY) WORKPLACE
Clean work area; no trash, debris, dirt
Arrange tools & materials for easy access
Remove items not needed for current work
Discipline to maintain work area
Standard procedures performed routinely

MATERIALS QUALITY
Make sure production receives only good parts/material
- inspect and sort before production if necessary
- safety stock if required to keep production going

Better solution is to purchase only good parts/material
- supplier (maker, distributor, etc.) inspects, sorts

Best solution is maker produces only good parts/material
- i.e. maker has effective quality systems

COMMUNICATION
People are most effective when they know what's going on
Interactive visual tools are useful to:
- inform and provide direction
- initiate improvement action (quality, performance, safety, etc.)
- resolve problems (quality, performance, safety, etc.)

Visual systems can be supplemented by reports and other after-the-fact data analyses

REQUIREMENTS COMPLIANCE
Document plans to achieve compliance
- all activities: design→production→delivery→support

Document attainment of compliance
- actual compliance evidence may be contained in separate records

CUSTOMER SUPPORT

Complete documentation for customer
- use, maintenance, disposal instructions
- information to answer any reasonable question

Rapid response to customer:
- questions, inquiries for information
- requests for assistance

**Quality Is Harmony;
In A State Of True Harmony,
The Least Energy Is Expended**

PRODUCT REQUIREMENTS

Thinking it might be useful, I have listed below the categories of product requirements information that we use at the plant. We endeavor to design a product that will meet the requirements throughout its life cycle. Requirements categories for a different company would depend on its products or services and its circumstances.

Description: basically outline or narrative of key information about the product

Function: what product is or does under what conditions; definition of satisfactory functionality; standard, optional features

Appearance, aesthetics

Cost: life cycle – acquisition, operation, maintenance, etc.

Performance: how well it must do what it does, or be what it is, in quantitative measures

Physical attributes: dimensions, weight, balance, orientation, etc.

Operation: who, when, where, how

Materials: function, performance, approved/prohibited, etc.

Surface treatments: finishes, coatings, etc.–exterior, interior

Logistics: how product will be handled, transported, stored, etc.

Integrity: reliability, destructibility, longevity, etc.

Maintenance & repair: who, what, when, where, how

Environmental impact: during operation, maintenance, and so on through final product disposition

Safety: to all, under all circumstances

Product revisions and upgrades

Additional special requirements (customer order, contract, etc.)

Testing, validation, and acceptance

Documentation: customer, third party, others

DESIGN FOR PRODUCTION

Product designs not only must meet requirements, they have to be manageable through production, transport, and other activities until the product has been turned over to the customer. Here are techniques and criteria we apply to accomplish this goal (beyond the quality focus in my Journal). Other companies may find different things to be appropriate.

Process conformity: basic idea: ensure designs conform to known processes used to produce them (known processes include tested new processes as required for new designs)

Simplicity: minimize complexity and variation, such as number of different parts or processes required (especially those differing only in small ways)

Standards: do things the same proven way every time—part selection; single & module designs; dimensions & locations; treatments; joining methods; test procedures, etc.—everything you can think of

Efficiency: economical use of: space, resources (e.g. power); need for manipulation, transport; etc.

Durability: avoid designs that are physically fragile and unable to withstand normal handling

Completeness: minimize necessity for design decisions during production; ensure unambiguous process for making required decisions

Single source   minimize necessity to synchronize multiple
for data: sources of the same production information

Ease of: process selection and performance; accessibility for processing, testing; performing every task

Flexibility: maximize capability to incorporate feedback, adapt to potential changes in design standards, processes, etc.

Balance: work content & packaging in standard amounts

Clarity: easy to comprehend, e.g. meaningful nomenclature, pictorial presentation—facilitate rapid clear understanding; minimize possibility of incorrect or multiple interpretations

Safety: eliminate, or significantly reduce, possibility of injury

Tolerances: for variances: design elements to specifications, production imperfections, etc.

Criticism Comes Easier
Than Craftsmanship

Fear Less; Hope More
Whine Less; Breathe More
Talk Less; Say More

PRODUCTION REMINDERS

When I reflected on the cat furniture project, I realized that its outcome had depended on successful integration of quality tools and tools for on-time low-cost production (to which I had been introduced during the shelf building project). To supplement my quality Journal, I prepared a list of key elements of production management beyond quality that I wanted to remember as I proceeded with improving quality at the plant. Here is that list.

Production Plan

Describes anticipated production, time frames, and resources required to achieve output

Establishes framework within which specific items can be produced as needed to satisfy actual demand

Includes surge capacity; avoids abrupt transitions in output or resource levels between time periods (balanced flow)

Prepared in several levels of detail and time horizons

Processes

Designed for efficiency and short cycle time
- both dedicated and flexible resources available (facilities, equipment, workforce)
- compact adaptable layout (minimal transport)
- minimal movement; all motion value-added
- rapid flow; production in small quantities
- balanced flow; balanced process work content
- concurrent & overlapping operations
- minimal setup/preparation time
- other techniques as appropriate

Focused application of technology
Eliminate safety risks
Eliminate possibility of undesirable environmental effects

Workforce

Highly qualified
Cross-trained; adaptable
Specific skills assigned to specific tasks with specific output
Dynamic reallocation as needed to meet goals

Production Release and Control

Production authorized as required to support actual production start in using process
Production to fit within resource plan framework, including surge capacity, or resource plan to be adjusted
Material and support provided to meet actual production starts
Goals established: measurable units per time period— tangible output, efficiency, etc.
Performance to goals continually monitored

Communication

Keep people fully informed, participating where possible
During production: continuous, interactive with workforce
Simple is good: graphs, drawings, other visuals
Complete timely information flow:
  – to production: plans & schedules; production orders;
    production work details; goals; other data as useful
  – during production: tasks, status, problems, actions
  – from production: results (many forms)
After the fact: analyses, other reports–detail and summary
Basic thought: communicate extensively, but do not burden
  people with information they can't use

Problem Response

Widespread immediate notification (alert system)
Rapid and decisive response
Actions taken to correct problem and avoid recurrence
  (something needs to be done differently)
Recovery plans developed if goals missed
Problem analyzed; root cause determined and eliminated

Material Control

Material acquired, stored, and distributed based on production
  plan and production order release
Quality and quantity validated before issue to production
Objective for outside suppliers: excellence of management and
  results equivalent to that demanded of internal production

Production Improvements

Always possible, in either leaps or incremental steps
Need to be managed; implemented with cautious haste

Facilities, Equipment, Tools, Supplies

Requirements driven by production plan
Acquired and employed as consistent with leadtimes and
    release of production work
Maintained to always be available when required

*There Is Nothing Kept From You
That You Have Not Kept From Yourself*

*Courage Is Not Absence Of Fear;
It Is Being Afraid And Going Ahead Anyway*

EPILOGUE

After the cat furniture project, I was back in Sandy's good graces. She showed me a summary of effective manufacturing principles, ***Ten Commandments of Manufacturing Excellence***, that she prepared after the earlier shelf project. I was inspired to create the following summary of quality principles.

It Is Wisdom Which Is Seeking Wisdom

TEN RULES OF QUALITY

☆ Believe in quality; quality can't be achieved by pretense

☆ Understand all requirements the product must satisfy through its entire life cycle; validate that it does so

☆ Define unambiguous specifications for meeting requirements; develop and validate a design that meets specs and can be produced, and used, without error

☆ Get quality people, equipment, and other resources; despite the fable, you can't spin straw into gold

☆ Use processes to produce, deliver, and support the product that are as error-proofed as possible

☆ Process variance is acceptable if it can be controlled within a range that still results in 100% defect-free products

☆ For processes where errors remain a possibility, thoroughly inspect process output to ensure its acceptability

☆ Apply quality principles to external suppliers; correcting someone else's mistakes is a poor way to start production

☆ Communicate incessantly; ignorance and delay are deadly enemies of quality

☆ Continually evaluate product quality to determine where and how it could be taken to a higher level

A Small Spark May Start A Great Fire

DISCUSSION GUIDE

Bayrock Press, publishers of this book, asked me if I would mind if they developed a few discussion questions for readers of my account of the cat furniture project. Including potentially embarrassing questions like whether I had done the right thing in certain situations. The new Joe said, of course, that was fine.

Therefore, here are some questions that draw on events in the story in order to stimulate thinking about quality and how to achieve it. I also encourage individuals and discussion groups to develop their own questions and explore the topic of quality thoroughly from all perspectives.

1. In Joe's first meeting with Sandy and Ralph to discuss the cat furniture project, he observes that high quality products are more competitive and more profitable (pages 10-12). Ralph comments that efficient production and high quality are highly integrated (pages 13-14). Do you agree with these comments? Does your organization? Would your organization benefit by following these principles? Are there situations when these principles might be less true than other situations?

2. Several issues arise during production of the prototype scratching post (pages 24-33). Joe revises the design so it matches production capabilities and is easier to produce using standard parts and processes. Give examples of these or similar issues in your organization. How should they be dealt with? What can you do to improve handling of such issues? Does your organization have a formal "Design for Production" program? Would it benefit from such a program or improving the current program? How could such a program be kicked off or improved?

3. Joe improves production instructions for the prototype scratching post and Team 2's climbing tree (pages 37-39). How do you feel about his standard instructions and content of production instructions (page 133)? Do you have additional ideas for your organization? How could your organization's instructions for task performance be improved? Who would need to be involved to make such improvements? How could that be made to happen?

4. On pages 41-42, Zeb and Roger have a heated discussion about quality of the cat condo on Team 3's prototype. What do you think about the solution they and Joe agree to? Does your organization have similar problems? Could they benefit from Joe's ideas? What is the role of inspection in your organization? Are completed tasks inspected for quality and identification of rework before subsequent tasks are performed? Is defective work ever sent on to the next process without correction? What could be done about that? Are Joe's views on Inspection/ Test (page 134) appropriate for your organization?

5. On page 55, Mickey is incapacitated by toxic gases from the carpeting adhesive. What do you think about this incident and Joe's solution? Does your organization strive

to make processes completely safe? Do you think they should? From this event and the later incident with the table saw (page 100), we see Joe believes higher quality is achieved with safe processes. Is this a reasonable belief?

6. On Sunday morning (pages 65-74), Joe finally defines product requirements information, which he summarizes in his Journal on page 132 and describes further on pages 139-140 as Product Requirements. Does your organization determine the requirements information Joe recommends? Should they? How could your organization improve processes for determining product requirements? What would they do first?

7. In his Journal, on page 132, Joe summarizes his views on how product design should be conducted in order for a product to meet its requirements. Does your organization employ a process with features similar to what he suggests? How could the design process be improved? What actions could be taken in the near term to improve the process?

8. Team 2 has a problem with quality of purchased brackets and screws (pages 81-82). They work out solutions, which Joe generalizes to "Materials Quality" principles. What are your organization's policies regarding purchased material quality? Are they effective? How could they be improved?

9. Joe states that quality of resources (people, tools, etc.) is critical to quality of output, and he has ideas for attaining high resource quality (pages 46-47, 84-87, 135). What do you think of his opinion of resource quality and approach to getting it? Does your organization have high (or at least adequate) quality of resources? If not, what could be done?

10. Joe believes error-proofing processes is the best road to quality (page 134). His views on error-proofed processes are developed through incidents with the dangling cat toy (pages 88-90) and the carpet glueing pattern (pages 102-105). What do you think of Joe's views? Give examples of error-proofing in your organization. And failure to error-proof. What could you do to reduce the possibility of errors in processes you are involved with?

11. Throughout the weekend Joe is bedeviled by delays and costs caused by poor quality. Does this happen in your organization? Give examples. Does your organization believe that achieving quality saves cost and time, or instead costs money and time? Are there cases of both? What would be a good example of poor quality impacting schedule and cost? How could this be corrected?

12. Joe's "Design for Production" principles (pages 133, 141-142) include advanced thoughts for how designs affect work flow, based on incidents with customer change orders (page 79) and last-minute schedule changes (pages 91-98). Does your organization encounter similar problems? Do they look at product design as contributing either to flow problems or improved flow? How could you facilitate a dialogue about this topic?

13. Sandy convinces Joe (pages 105-106, 136) that requirements compliance needs to be verified, no matter how good the design and execution processes for satisfying requirements. Do you think this is always true, or can it be overkill? How does your organization verify that customer requirements have or have not been attained (other than customer complaints)? Could requirements compliance be improved? How could that be done or initiated?

14. Based on Zeb's efforts to clean and organize Team 3's workplace (pages 49, 74, 111-112), Joe documents his thoughts on achieving a quality workplace (pages 113, 135). Do you agree with him that workplace quality affects product quality? What is required to improve workplace quality in your organization? Are Joe's thoughts adequate, or should additional things be considered?

15. By mid-Sunday afternoon, production is flowing so smoothly that the teams elect to ramp up the production rate (pages 113-117) to make more cat furniture. Widespread use is made of visual communication tools, which Joe documents (page 136) as well as the necessity for written communication. Are these or similar tools deployed in your organization? Can you think of ways to improve quality through improving communication?

16. After people take their cat furniture home, and then talk about it with friends, Joe finds that his weekend project has an ongoing life (pages125-128). He summarizes his "Customer Support" thoughts in his journal (page 137). Do you think that his thoughts on documentation for customers are accurate? How about his opinions on rapid response to customer requests? Would you change or add anything? How could your organization improve support of current and potential customers?

17. Ongoing improvement, based on input from several sources, is the final lesson that Joe lists under "Basic Principles" in his journal (page 131). What is your view of this and the other basic principles? What would you add or subtract? How can you help to communicate basic principles in your organization and get everybody on board? What would happen if various people in the organization

believed in different quality principles instead of in the same things?

18. Considering all of the quality points made by Joe, which points stick in your mind as the most important? What is the most important quality issue for your organization to work on? What is the most important quality issue for you personally to work on? Which quality tools should you and/or the organization work on first? How would you and/or the organization go about taking the next steps?

19. What are the major messages or themes of the book? Do you agree with them? Do you think your organization agrees with them? If not, why not?

20. How important is high quality for your organization's products? Should quality be improved? If not, why not? If so, make a list of potential actions to improve the quality of the products.

The Finger Pointing At The Moon
Is Not The Moon

A Good Roof Keeps Out The Rain

FINAL THOUGHTS

Parts of this tale probably seem very real. However, we admit to inventing the whole thing. Characters, events, places, and so on, are all imaginary. Cat furniture exists, of course, but all comments about it—and about producers, sellers, and users of it—are made by imaginary characters and are not real outside of their imaginary world, nor do they refer to anything in the real world that you and we inhabit. Other obviously real things, like Starbucks, are used in fictional and hopefully complimentary ways. Throughout the book, if you thought we were talking about something which really existed, that simply means you are a creative reader and we wrote a pretty good story.

The sayings, as far as we know, are either original or timeless and incapable of attribution to a unique source. If you have other thoughts, please let us know through Bayrock Press.

Thanks for reading our book.

Bill Miller   Vicki Schenk

Lead By Serving

ABOUT THE AUTHORS

Bill Miller and Vicki Schenk are authors and management consultants. They have extensive experience in business, from working in all functions to running companies. Bill is the author of ***America's Management Challenge***, a selection of the Executive Book Club. Bill and Vicki co-authored the bestseller ***All I Need To Know About Manufacturing I Learned In Joe's Garage***, used by thousands of organizations worldwide to improve performance. They can be contacted through their company's website www.wmillerco.com.

A Good Deed Is Like A Gift

ORDERING INFORMATION

This book, and other books in the *Joe's Garage* series, can be purchased through regular book selling channels, either on-line or stores.

For bulk purchases or special needs, contact Bayrock Press directly by telephone at 888-670-7625 or through their website www.bayrockpress.com.

Language Is Metaphor